NO CASH?
NO PROBLEM!™

HOW TO GET WHAT YOU WANT IN BUSINESS AND LIFE, WITHOUT USING CASH

DAVE WAGENVOORD
& ALI PERVEZ

NEW YORK

NO CASH? NO PROBLEM!™

How to get what you want in business and life, without using cash

ISBN 978-1-61448-361-8 paperback
ISBN 978-1-61448-362-5 eBook
Library of Congress Control Number: 2012945673
Black Belt Publishing an Imprint of Morgan James Publishing.

Morgan James Publishing
The Entrepreneurial Publisher
5 Penn Plaza, 23rd Floor, New York City, New York 10001
(212) 655-5470 office • (516) 908-4496 fax
www.MorganJamesPublishing.com

Barter? Most people don't even see it on the radar.
The smart ones do!

– Jay Abraham
World's Leading Marketing Authority

To my amazing wife, Ayesha
- Ali Pervez

To my business and life partner, Lola Wagenvoord
- Dave Wagenvoord

contents

acknowledgments

I would like to first thank Dave Wagenvoord for taking me "under his wing" and mentoring me in the art of barter. Although all the examples and case studies in this book are real transactions that Dave Wagenvoord has done, writing this book has allowed me to be a fly on the wall and gain an inside view of what barter trade is all about and its incredible potential. Dave, you are an amazing person and mentor. Thank you for stretching my mind and imagination beyond what I thought was possible and for teaching me a whole new way of thinking.

Even though I wrote about barter in my book Get Your Black Belt in Marketing (www.blackbeltinmarketing.com; move #62), and I knew then that barter, or trade, was used by some of the world's greatest marketers, I didn't really understand how powerful it really was! I said in my book that each move could be a book in itself, and this book clearly shows this to be true. Well, who better to learn barter from than the master of trade himself and the world's greatest bartering expert, Dave Wagenvoord. I thank you, sir, for allowing me to pick your brain and for your patience in teaching me over the last two years. It was certainly challenging doing the East Coast–West Coast trips and vice versa. But we did it! Your wisdom will now be passed on to generations to come.

I hope I have been a good student. I may be a master of marketing, but I have had the opportunity to learn from the Grand Master of Bartering. Thanks again for expanding my horizons and introducing me to a whole new world that is now only limited by my imagination and creativity. Now that I am able to connect the dots, my life will never be the same again.

I would like to also acknowledge two of the greatest minds in marketing history, Jay Abraham and Jay Conrad Levinson, giants whose shoulders I have climbed on to launch my own marketing career. You are both amazing human beings. Thank you for passing on the love and passion for marketing to me. I hope I have been a good student and am able to continue to walk in your giant footsteps.

I would also like thank my wife, Ayesha, and two kids, Lina and Adeel, for letting me "go under" and disappear into another world to get this book completed. Writing is never an easy task. I love you more than you know for having the belief and confidence in my ability and allowing me to follow my passion. You all are and will always be my real wealth and inspiration. Thanks especially to Ayesha for always being so supportive and believing in me when no one else did. You never once stopped me from following my passion and dream of helping others with my marketing knowledge and talents, and my goal of making marketing fun, simple, and practical for everyone. Thank you—this book would not be possible without you. You took care of what needed to be taken care of while I was away traveling extensively and also working day and night on this book.

I would also like to thank the people who helped me revise this book and gave me invaluable feedback, including Vanessa Canoy in the Philippines, who stayed up many nights reading the initial manuscript and who graded me on each chapter; Eric McGill for giving me feedback on the initial manuscript; and Matt Clark in

Hollywood for putting his acting career aside to give me honest feedback on the initial manuscript from a whole new perspective! Matt, you are a true friend. I love you, man!

Special thanks to a special lady, Amanda Rooker, www.amanda-rooker.com, who is the chief editor of this book. We met by chance, but I was blessed to meet you. I really appreciate you!

I thank my mum who prays for me every day, hoping that I will one day become a "real marketing guru." Mum, I think I made it!

And of course, thanks to my mentor and very dear friend, David Hancock. I owe a great deal of my success to David, who always believed in me, even before I believed in myself. He truly is instrumental in who I have become. Thank you, sir! I hope I have made you proud. (It was a lot of hard work, and I am still learning!)

Finally, I thank you, the reader, for purchasing this book. I hope this is the book that you have been looking for, the book that finally changes your life by changing your thinking—as the only thing that can change your life is your thinking! This book is about creativity and thinking out of the box. After reading this book, you will start to see things differently, and I sincerely hope it helps you live the life of your dreams. Please read this book with an open mind, and you will get the most out of it. Thanks for your trust in me.

Your humble friend,

Ali Pervez

I'd like to thank my business and life partner, Lola Wagenvoord—aka Lola Jean, the Broadcast Queen; aka Lola O'Brien, the Irish Hawaiian. Lola is COO and general manager of our broadcast properties: WTAN-AM 1340, Tampa Bay; WDCF-AM 1350, Tampa Bay; WZHR-AM 1400, Tampa Bay; KLRG-AM 880 and FM 94.5, Little Rock, Arkansas; and KWAI-AM 1080, Honolulu, Hawaii.

Also, thanks to Jay Abraham, "the best marketing guru in the country, period," for helping me meet my coauthor, Ali Pervez, "author of a bestselling marketing book" and whose wife makes the best chicken pot pie in California. I'd also like to thank my dogs Gilda, Ragsdale, Roxie, and Holden—five hundred pounds of excitement and fun, without whose help this book would not have been possible. Down, boy!

Dave Wagenvoord

foreword
by Jay Conrad Levinson

I would like to congratulate both Dave and Ali for putting together such an outstanding book that finally explains what I believe is one of the most misunderstood, jealously guarded, but immensely profitable and fun ways of doing business. It's called barter trade— or just barter or trade, for short.

You are about to begin a journey of a lifetime that will get your creative juices flowing, because barter is really no more than a metaphor for creative and "out-of-the-box" thinking. You will soon begin to undertake a paradigm shift in the way you think, the way you do business, and the way you view life in general.

When done correctly, barter will improve the productivity and efficiency of your business. It can also multiply your buying power several fold by allowing you to buy goods and services at 50–60 percent discount off full retail prices, and it can give you immense leverage—at no additional cost and very little effort!

Using barter trade, you can nearly always get better terms, credits, and discounts than you would normally by paying cash, and more time to pay. You nearly always pay on a deferred basis for what you want and also get it interest free. And that's just the start! A "barter dollar" is usually worth more than a cash dollar! You can pay your employees or vendors, or do anything you would normally do with cash, by using barter or trade.

When you use barter to augment your current business, you really can't go wrong. Of all the marketing tools I know, I would say that barter is the best way to get more clients by far.

Barter is a weapon for Guerrilla Marketers. It is one of the most powerful marketing tools that few people understand.

The people you are about to meet are world experts in their own right. Dave Wagenvoord has traded over half a billion dollars in trade credits. He is a legend and has traded cars, motor homes, boats, real estate, and more. And he's traded with giants such as FedEx, DHL, Four Seasons, Marriott, KLM, and Sheraton, to mention just a few. His client list looks like the who's who of business.

Ali Pervez is a marketing expert whom I am sure you will continue to hear much more about. He has written two excellent books on marketing and is very passionate about the field. He is a very genuine, sincere, and compassionate human being.

Together they have simplified barter down to its essence and to a science that can give you predictable results.

But if barter is that good, why don't more people use it? I think it is because of a lack of education: either they don't know about it, or they don't know how to use it to gain maximum leverage for their business. So I am so happy that Dave and Ali have put this book together to finally remove the mystique and misunderstanding that seems to surround barter or trade. They have been able to simplify it so it may now reach a wider audience.

What surprises me is how little has been written about this subject, based on how powerful the concept is once you are able to master it. Maybe that is why only five hundred people in the world truly understand how to barter to gain maximum leverage.

Barter is an art as well as a science, and you will soon learn that it takes a lot of real finesse to put together a good barter deal. But when done correctly, the results can be prolific. Barter can totally change the course and destiny of any business. It could be the strategy that you have been looking for. You will also see examples of barter deals that have been done, and many case studies that clearly show the immense power that barter offers as a business and marketing tool. Barter, or trade, like a lot of very good principles, is very simple, and I think that it is its simplicity that intimidates people.

Once you master barter trade, you will only be limited by your imagination. And you will start living your life and business with a sense of possibility. You will become an expansive and exponential thinker versus a lateral one. At its most basic, barter will improve your margins, lower your expenses, and bring you new, unfound business opportunities. At its best, it will totally change the way you look at business and life.

Without taking the tagline from AT&T, barter will make you "rethink what is possible," once you have read and studied the real-world case studies in this book. I am truly excited for what you are about to learn. Barter principles have certainly changed my life, and I sincerely hope they change yours also. Barter trade will allow you to be more, see more, and do a whole lot more with your time, effort, and money! The type of barter deals you will be putting together will soon only be limited by the power of your imagination. With barter trade, the sky is not the limit; it really is just the beginning. Welcome to a new universe!

—Jay Conrad Levinson

Father of Guerrilla Marketing and author of the Guerrilla Marketing series, which has sold more than 21 million copies in 63 languages

disclaimer

We make no claim or reference to any specific tax implications of barter using this book. Each case is unique. Please consult your tax advisor or tax professional for any tax-related or legal questions.

Names of certain companies have been removed for confidentiality reasons.

Results from barter trades may vary. We make no claim or guarantee of any results.

introduction

Sometimes the questions are complicated and the
answers are simple.

Dr. Seuss

"No cash? No problem!" Can this really be true? Can you really get what you want in business or life without reaching for your checkbook, pulling out your wallet, or even swiping your credit card? The answer is yes—if you are prepared to change the way you think and start to use your time, energy, and imagination instead of using cash.

In this groundbreaking book, you will learn how to get what you want in life without using cash or smoke and mirrors, just common sense. The techniques you are about to learn are time-tested and proven, and used by some of the world's smartest marketers, business folks, and individuals. They know something that you need to know, and that is that you really don't need money, or so-called cash, to get what you want. You can just as easily trade your products, services, time, talents, knowledge, imagination, inventory, or expertise instead of trading cash. And use creativity as your new currency!

The question is, why should you pay for it when you could trade for it, using "old dollars" that you have already spent on things that you already have in your possession? You are about to embark on a journey of a lifetime that will hopefully change the way you think about business and life, and find out why barter really is just so much smarter.

You will learn a time-tested and proven strategy for wealth generation that has been used by some of the wealthiest people in the world for centuries. It is a secret that is said to be known to less than five hundred people around the world. These are people who are "in the know" about how to create wealth very quickly.

This same secret was used by a major international hotel chain to buy millions of dollars' worth of advertising without spending a penny, and it was the strategy used to save one of Beverly Hills' top hotels from bankruptcy. It's a tool so powerful that it was also used to build the world's largest cruise line and the world's largest home-shopping network company—and made the founders exceptionally wealthy in the process, putting them on the Forbes' list of high-net-worth individuals.

The secret is how to use barter trade—or trade, for short—as a business or personal tool to purchase goods and services you need without paying cash, and in the process gain immense leverage in any transaction you may care to make. Bartering occurs when you exchange goods or services without exchanging money. In fact, in a true barter exchange, it is actually illegal to exchange any money.

Barter is certainly not new; it actually predates money. Today barter trade is estimated to be a six-billion-dollar business in the United States alone. Barter is the same as money; the only difference is that you don't pay with money! In ancient times, when people would trade with each other, a hunter, for example, would trade his catch for goods with a local business merchant.

Without knowing it, we all trade every day, but it does not appear on your radar unless you are highly trained in marketing. If you are employed, you are simply trading your time for money. The other most popular and unnoticed form of trade is "time for time" trade. Have you heard the following statements in your family?

- "I cooked dinner; now you need to do the dishes."
- "I'll clean the room if you'll help me with my assignment."
- "I'll wash the car if you collect my laundry."

These are all barter trades. Now you have made the connection!

Trade or barter may be the oldest form of commerce, but what most people don't know or realize is how extensively it is still being used as a wealth-building strategy.

The only reason that cash replaced barter as a means of commerce is that it was more convenient and universal. Cash deals are instantaneous; barter deals take longer but are a lot more profitable.

Barter can be used to pay bills, employees, and acquire and get new clients—all ethically and legally, of course. In fact, it is also the best loyalty program you could develop for your company. It can do everything you would do with cash, and so much more, to enrich your business and personal life.

Barter is a creative and fun way to move unsold, unused, or excess inventory at full retail value. In fact, you can often get a better deal on trade than you can using conventional cash! You will soon see many real-world case studies and examples of how all this is all done.

McHUMOR.com by T. McCracken

"I'm sorry, but you're being
replaced by an abacus."

The answer that you are looking for is right underneath your feet and in the palm of your hands, if you are prepared to change your thinking and start offering your goods and services as a form of payment versus paying cash!

In this book, you will meet two legendary and world-class marketing experts in their own right who will take you by the hand and show you how a barter trade really works. This book will soon become your personal blueprint, road map, and manual for success, and something that you will want to keep with you at all times to help you stay in your newfound mindset.

It will change the way that you think about business and hopefully life in general, and it will open up your mind and imagination to what is really possible if you allow yourself the freedom to think creatively and out-of-the-box.

In Part I, you will be grounded in the principles of barter trade: what it is, how it works, and why it works so well. Then in Part II, you will be taken into real-world case studies and transactions and see how companies like American Express, Mazda, Chrysler, and many others have all used this incredibly powerful tool to leverage their marketing spend.

The book will cover both B2B (business to business) and C2C (consumer to consumer) trading. So if you are a small- to medium-sized business owner doing B2B or B2C, you will learn how to grow your sales without growing your marketing budget, using strategies that will bring you the much-deserved success you have been looking for, and learn how to finally work smarter, not harder.

If you are a consumer, you will learn how to trade your excess time or talents to get what you need, without reaching for your wallet, check card, or checkbook.

If you are the owner of a large corporation, you will learn how to get much more out of your marketing spend than you ever have thought possible. You will learn how to recycle 100 percent of your marketing spend right back into your own business. Most businesses are lucky if they get single-digit returns on their advertising. But using barter you can get 100 percent return on your advertising. You will see how all this is done with real-world case studies.

As economies around the world weaken, a new—or really, a very old—form of commerce makes its comeback, which is barter.

Barter transactions have been used by governments for centuries: all major governments have a department of "trade" and industry. And they understand how powerful trade can be. Now it is your turn to use this tool for your businesses or your life. Barter trades, when done correctly, are immensely powerful and lucrative and are always part of any successful business's portfolio. Barter trade provides a maximum ROI: return on *intelligence*. Because it is simply a very smart way to do business.

Learn this little-known secret used by the world's most successful corporations and marketing wizards, and you will soon start to enjoy the benefits that others have known about for centuries.

Unlike other books, this book is not based on potential or theory. It is based on facts and actual deals that have been done by WAGI Advertising. This way you will clearly see how trade works in the real world. After reading this book, you will be ready to do your first barter-trade deal. We hope that you may even do your first deal before you finish the book!

The book is about helping you step out of your comfort zone and into your natural creative zone, where you start to see opportunities where others see problems and develop what we call "x-ray" vision.

In 1995, Marc Ostrofsky purchased business.com for $150,000. Most people thought he was crazy, but he was able to see something that others were not able to see, which was the power and potential of the Internet. He subsequently sold business.com for $7,500,000 just four years later in 1999. The sale landed in the *Guinness Book of World Records* for the largest amount anyone had ever paid for a website address. They did not think he was so crazy then! He had x-ray vision. He was able to see the opportunity and was an out-of-the-box thinker.

We don't know if you will do what Marc was able to do, but after reading this book, we know you will be well on your way to being an out-of-the-box, expansive thinker.

Dave Wagenvoord is a legend in his own right and one of the icons of barter trade. He is often referred to as the father of radio barter. Having been involved in trade for over forty years, he has done over half a billion dollars' worth of barter trade.

Here are just a few of some of his amazing barter feats:

- He traded 900 Chrysler Imperials in six weeks. Only 1,100 were manufactured that year.

- He traded 16,000 guitars for Yamaha for more than $2,000,000 worth of radio advertising.

- He traded $5,000,000 worth of DHL Air Courier credits for television in a matter of months.

- He traded for advertising on hundreds of radio stations for ten years for Carnival Cruise Lines.

- He built Channel 26 TV in New Orleans, which is now owned by the Chicago Tribune.

- He owned the Peter Lawford home on the beach in Santa Monica that was used by President Kennedy and known as the "Western White House." This was originally built as the home of Louis B. Mayer, the founder of Metro-Goldwyn-Mayer, and is the birthplace of the concept of the Academy Awards. Dave traded for the house and much of its contents.

- He purchased a radio station in Northern California and paid 60 percent of the down payment in furniture trade credits.

- He bought $1,000,000 worth of network airtime from a bankruptcy court in one of the wildest and most profitable "little" barter deals of all time.

- Dave and Lola Wagenvoord currently own six radio stations: three in Tampa Bay, Florida; one in Honolulu, Hawaii; and two in Little Rock, Arkansas.

- His clients have included:

Best Western Hotels	Avis	Carl's Jr
Sheraton Hotels	Hawaiian Tropic Sutan Oil	Mutual Broadcasting
Outrigger Hotels	Costa Cruise Line	Levitz Furniture
Beverly Wilshire Hotel	Regal Cruise Line	General Rent-A-Car
L'Ermitage Hotel Beverly Hills	Pearl Cruise Line	Coty Perfume
Carnival Cruise Line	Aer Lingus airlines	Aeroflot
Aero Mexico	Royal Caribbean Cruise	Carnival Airlines
KLM	Silver Club Hotel Reno Nevada	Wittenauer Watches
Continental Airlines	Mexicana Airlines	Landmark Hotel Las Vegas
RCA	Air France	Hawaiian Air
Citizen Watches	Curtis Publishing	Surf Resorts Hawaii
Turner Broadcasting	Lufthansa Air	MGM Grand Las Vegas
NBC Radio	TWA	Sahara Hotel Las Vegas
Budget Rent-A-Car	Samsung	Eton Radios

And Over 5,000 radio and TV stations in America

Ali Pervez is one of America's leading marketing educators, with over twenty-five years of hands-on, practical global marketing experience.

He is the bestselling marketing author of *Get Your Black Belt in Marketing* (www.blackbeltinmarketing.com). He holds undergraduate and postgraduate degrees in science, and he was awarded an MBA with a distinction project in marketing from the Manchester Business School in the UK. He was also awarded two Vice President awards for Outstanding Contribution in Marketing within his first year at Abbott Laboratories. He is a Fellow of the Royal Society of Chemistry, founder of The Black Belt Marketing Consulting Group, and a much-sought-after international marketing consultant.

For the first time in history, Dave and Ali will reveal to you how you can unleash the power of barter trade in your business and use it to enrich your life. After reading this book, you will soon find that "No cash? No problem!" will hold true for you also!

PART 1:
Understanding barter trade

chapter one

— 1 —

The Ancient Wisdom of Our Ancestors Returns

Once the mind has been stretched by a new idea, it will never again return to its original shape.

Oliver Wendell Holmes Jr.

"No cash? No problem!" Can this be real? How can it be possible? Can you truly have "cashless transactions?" The answer is yes—if you are prepared to adopt a new mindset and start to think about paying for the goods and services that you need with goods and services that you already have in your possession and have already paid for! Or basically return to the ancient practice of barter trade—or trade, for short—which is a concept that predates money. The answer you have been looking for is right under your nose and in the palm of your hand. You have just not made the connection.

Welcome to a new type of bank that trades in a whole new type of currency.

Although we have been conditioned to think that cash is king, it is not really true. What really is king are the products, services, skills, and talents you have that can be traded for products and services you may need. The only reason that we have "cash" as you know it today is for convenience and to make trade universal across borders. And the only reason you have an attachment to cash is not for

3

what it is, which is really just paper or coins, but for all the goodies that cash can buy for you! Or what cash can do. But you can do the same transaction without cash. If you have inventory or products that are going to waste, you can trade these for something you may want or need, versus trashing them. Some folks call this recycling; others call it optimization, or going green. Either way, it is smart to take something that has no value, or shortly about to have no value, and convert it into a valuable asset, or something that you may need or want and can use immediately.

We agree that you may not be able to control the economy, but you can certainly learn to take advantage of it. And in today's economy where cash is short, barter thrives, as barter is the only way to get what you want without exchanging any cash.

Savvy investors have known for a long time that down economies are a perfect time to make money, and nearly 60 percent of the Fortune 500 companies were founded in recessions. Apple, Microsoft, Disney, and Charles Schwab all have their roots in down economies; they were able to see opportunities and invested when others were fearful.

In the same way, barter allows you to take advantage of our current economic condition and to thrive and prosper in it. How can this be? Because barter trade's roots lie in tough economic times.

Barter will allow you to finance your transactions without ever having to go to the bank, offering any securities, or showing any credit history. There is a tremendous gold mine today for creative people who are prepared to think outside of the box and are seriously willing to look at barter as a creative finance tool for their business, or even their personal life.

When you think of barter, you may think of a farmer paying a doctor in chickens for their services, which is most probably how it all started. But barter has evolved today into a real art and is used extensively not only by individuals, but also by highly successful businesses and even nations to overcome the problem of weak currencies. For example, today every major Western government has a department of trade and industry. And many third-world countries survive by trading commodities with other nations.

"Don't worry, the first 30 years
of farming are the hardest."

There are thousands of trade clubs that exist around the world that we will soon be talking about, each which trades millions of dollars of goods and services daily. Even Amazon will trade with you! You can trade your old books, electronics, and other items for an Amazon gift card! Just visit www.amazon.com/trade. So barter is happening every day around you as we speak, and we hope this book will open up your mind and imagination to a whole new way (or, really, old way) of doing commerce that is now back on the rise!

Trade today is a highly sophisticated and advanced creative financing tool that is both known and used by some of the most successful and well-known business enterprises and entrepreneurs around the world—household names that you would recognize immediately. Companies like Sheraton, KLM, Best Western, TWA, Samsung, and NBC use and have used barter as part of their business-building strategies.

This all leads us to the real secret to creating wealth in your life or business, which is:

If you don't have money, you invest your time. If you don't have time, you invest your money.

Most conventional books on finance are about investing your money in the stock market, real estate, or other investment vehicles as a wealth-building strategy. This also is a book on finance, but creative finance—for situations in which you don't have money to invest! In these cases, you invest your excess time, talents, and inventory.

Although you may think that barter trade is no longer used or may even be primitive, you will shortly see how so far from the truth this really is. We assure you that barter trade today is alive, well, and flourishing as a highly advanced form of commerce. Barter trade clubs use highly sophisticated software and operate just like banks. Today you can do virtually anything you would normally do with cash on trade, or without cash!

Most merchants that take or offer trade have a trade logo from the organization or trade club they are a part of, shown at their place of business. You may have not noticed them. They look similar to Visa or MasterCard logos.

Bottom line: trade is not only back in style but on the rise, and it is your turn to catch the wave.

In life we make money by solving other people's problems for profit or pay: profit if we are in business, and pay if we are an employee. Barter is simply another vehicle for exchanging goods and services, and another way to solve each other's problems.

The purpose of this book is to educate you on the power and potential of barter trade, and open your mind and imagination to what is really possible if you truly embrace it as a way of life, and adopt a new way of thinking about how to solve problems.

As Tom Peters, one of the world's leading management consultants, says in his books *In Search of Excellence* and *Re-Imagine! Business Excellence in a Disruptive Age*, "Nothing is unimaginable." We totally agree.

But before we start our journey together, let's lay out the basics of barter or trade and remove what we believe is one of the biggest mistakes, misunderstandings, and even misconceptions that people have when it comes to trade: they think that barter is a one-way exchange, or maybe is free. Not true!

> Barter very simply means that instead of paying
> for what you want with cash, you are exchanging
> value for equivalent value.

Barter is not rocket science. It very simply means that instead of paying for what you want with cash, you are exchanging value for value, which is your time, talents, or goods and services for other people's time, talents, or goods and services. Barter doesn't mean that you are getting stuff for free; you are simply exchanging value for equivalent value.

Two things need to happen for a barter exchange to work effectively:

1. You need to have something to barter—i.e., something that is valuable to someone else. You are not getting anything for FREE. You are just not paying for it with cash!

2. You must honor your portion of the credit when they come to redeem their portion.

> The mathematical equation for barter is very simple: I give you x, and you give me y in return.

Regarding the first point, the mathematical equation for barter is very simple: I give you x, and you give me y in return. So, theoretically, $x = y$ in barter. Both have equivalent value. And only when $x = y$ can you say you have a "fair trade." And the second part of the deal is that you must stand by the credit that you offer. For example, if you offer someone food at your restaurant for plumbing services, you must honor the credit you issued when they come in to eat. And likewise they must honor the plumbing services credit they gave you, when you need to fix that broken pipe!

Barter transactions require the highest degree of integrity.

Barter or trade is the way that our ancestors did business, and it worked for centuries. They knew the barter trade equation: $x = y$.

 # INSIDE SECRET #1

Life is about problem solving. Barter is a tool that allows you to solve problems without using any cash. Money—or cash, as we know it—is just a means of representing value. But this value can be just as equally represented directly with your products, goods, services, time, and talents!

The only reason that we use "money" or "cash" today is that it is both convenient and universal. This is all good, but the problem is when cash is short, we find ourselves struggling to do commerce. But it does not need to be like this if we think creatively and understand that barter is also a currency.

The problem is that we are so entrenched in the cash-based economy that we forget that there is actually another "cashless" economy that has worked successfully for generations before us and can just as easily work well today.

If this is the case, then why do more people not consider barter or trade as an alternative to solve everyday problems? We think it is for several reasons, which we will address in the next chapter. But the primary reason, like everything in life, is bad conditioning: the lack of education and knowledge. Again, the goal of this book is to challenge you to think out of the box and help you maximize your potential in ways that you never thought possible. We want you to break through your conventional and linear thinking patterns and give you permission to barter—and yes, it is perfectly legal! In fact, the IRS actually encourages you to barter and has a dedicated Barter Tax Center, which we will talk about later. There is no law or restriction preventing two parties from bartering or trading with each other, as long as they both see equal value in the exchange. And take care of the necessary paperwork.

We hope that the many real-world examples that we will present to you will become your wake-up call to finally break out of your traditional thinking and into your creative problem-solving skills. So you can get what you want and deserve in life. You will see many examples of how what started off as a simple trade deal ended up as billion-dollar enterprises. Both Carnival Cruise Lines and the Home Shopping Network grew out of very simple trade deals. Although nearly everyone has heard about barter, few truly understand how to use it to leverage marketing expenditure by issuing a "scrip" or your own currency. This is just one way barter or trade can be immensely powerful as a creative financing tool, as you get to set the terms, payments, interest rates, and more to meet your specific needs. More on this shortly.

Barter is your banker's worst nightmare, because when you start to use your goods and services as the currency, you don't really need any banker. Your banker prays that you never read this book!

Trade operates in the opposite way as cash. In cash transactions, the longer you take to pay, the more you end up paying in both interest charges and fees. In barter or trade, the longer you take to pay, the less you end up paying, because all of your credits are not likely to be used up immediately, and some may not be used at all due to a concept called breakage—which you will be learning about shortly. It is estimated that about 30 percent of all world trade is done using barter to overcome the issue of "soft curren-

---

FUN FACT

Manhattan Island was bought by the Dutch in 1626 from the Lenape Indian tribe in one of the greatest barter trades of the century—just a $24 trade in beads!

---

cies." Barter is not only the oldest way of doing business, but it is actually a lot more effective, efficient, and profitable than cash if done correctly.

Although you may think that cash offers a more secure way of doing commerce than barter, think again. The cash we use has no real value; it may not even be worth the paper it is printed on.

Our cash or currency today is not backed by anything. In the good old days, it was backed by gold, but President Nixon ended this on August 15, 1971, when United States currency was no longer tied to gold reserves. So we are, in essence, "trading" paper today that has nothing behind it. Cash, as we know it, is really an illusion!

We promise you that once you have finished reading this book, you will know exactly how barter trade is done. You will learn one of the best-kept and most jealously guarded secrets in the marketing world, said to be known to only five hundred people. The concept of using trade to leverage your marketing expenditures is now being called the secret of the century.

The most important thing to remember about trade is that the whole process starts with the right mindset:

 # INSIDE SECRET #2

Barter experts know that you don't have to pay for it. You can just as easily trade for it.

This book is about creative thinking! To be good at trading or bartering, you need to think of creative ways to solve real-world problems. The barter mindset is all about how to put the deals together: what does someone want, and what can you trade with them to get what you want?

Barter can be used to pay bills, employees, offset cash expenses, build a new sales channel for your business, buy a house or boat, book a holiday, or do basically anything that you would do with cash!

You are simply using your goods and services as the form of payment. It's not free; it is certainly not illegal. It's just creative and smart! And all of this can be done without you or the person you are trading with having to reach for their wallet, checkbook, or check card.

Once you grasp the concept of barter or trade, you will start to see more, be more, and do more with the time, money, talents, goods, or services you already have in your possession. We promise you that sometime during this book the light will go off, you will have that "aha moment," and you will put the book down and rush off to do your first trade deal. Trust us, it will happen. We are so excited about what you are about to learn!

Barter or trade is also a way to generate cash very quickly, because what you receive in trade can be sold on the open market for cash, something that we barter experts call "cash conversion," which you will also learn about shortly.

 # INSIDE SECRET #3

Barter or trade not only saves cash, but also can generate it for you! All using your excess time, talents, and inventory!

Now you can see why individuals and businesses across the world are now taking a very serious look at barter as a way to build their business portfolio, enhance their bottom line, and create a desirable lifestyle.

The Internet is a perfect medium for trade. You can trade with people around the world from the comfort of your desktop. We believe that the next generation of millionaires will be barter specialists running trading sites on the Internet.

Barter truly has the opportunity to turn your marketing both upside down and inside out as you move from conventional to creative marketing strategies. Put simply, barter gives your business incredible leverage, as opposed to conventional dollar-based expenditures. With barter, you can get what you want *without*:

- Asking for a line of credit from your bank

- Showing your balance sheet

- Offering any personal guarantees

- Borrowing from your friends or family

- Waiting! Which is critical if your business is on the verge of a financial crisis.

We have known businesses that could have been saved if they had understood the barter-trade strategies that we will cover in this book. At the same time, we know businesses that have gone on to become multi-billion-dollar enterprises because of their understanding of these strategies (Carnival Cruise Line and Home Shopping Network being just two examples of this).

Barter trade allows you to literally set up a bank in a matter of seconds, without any government approval! And all legally, of course. We will give you very specific real-world examples of how all this is done.

Although most of the examples in this book relate to trading products and services for businesses' most precious asset (which is advertising), the principles are universal and can be applied to any business or life situation—if you adopt the mindset of the barter trader. We strongly believe that mindset is more important than method. Once you master the mindset, it literally can be applied to any area of your life, as you will become a creative and expansive thinker able to solve any business or life problem.

INSIDE SECRET #4

In barter you can trade whatever you want, if you have the mindset that someone needs what you have.

But we warn you in advance that what we are about to teach you may intimidate the linear thinker.

INSIDE SECRET #5

The "linear thinkers" amongst you will try to find a catch in barter, but we hate to disappoint you—there is none!

In fact, you will find that barter is the most ethical and honest way to do business. It has worked for centuries for our ancestors; why can't it work for you? We will be bold enough to say that if barter is not part of your business portfolio, you are actually losing money. And if it is not part of your life, you are missing out, because at any time, you can trade your excess time, capacity, or knowledge for something that you may need, without paying cash.

INSIDE SECRET #6

Barter, to us, is really about people helping people solve everyday problems, whereas conventional commerce is simply about profit. And that is why we love it so much.

FUN FACT

In ancient times, salt was hard to find and very valuable to people. Everybody wanted salt to flavor and preserve their food. So salt was used for money. In ancient Rome, the soldiers were paid with salt!

As you can see, we really love barter trade, because there is so much more to it than just making money, which conventional commerce is based on. Barter originally started out as a way for people to help people. And there is no reason why it cannot continue with that philosophy today.

You will shortly be leaving your current world that is limited by cash to enter a new world that does not require cash and allows you to gain endless purchasing power. But this will require work on your part to start to expand your mind and imagination and adopt a non-conventional perspective to life and commerce. Albert Einstein said,

"Imagination is more important than knowledge."

We think he was talking about barter trade! And once you see some of the barter trades that we have done, you will understand why.

Lack of money is a common excuse for not being creative enough.

If you think about marketing, it is simply a tool used to generate sales in the business world. There are really only two ways to market:

1. CONVENTIONAL MARKETING

a) Create perceived value for the product or service you wish to sell in the eyes of the purchaser, so they believe that they are getting more value than what they are paying in cash. The ultimate sales formula is:

Sales always occur when perceived value > price paid

b) Discount or liquidate it by doing a "closeout" or offering discounts or "fire sales." This is a quick and easy way to get rid of any goods or services you may have.

2. CREATIVE MARKETING

But how about trading (i.e., barter)? Use what you already have and have already paid for in "hard dollars," and trade this to get what you want or need. As you know now, "trade" does not mean getting something for free. You need to offer something of value and get something of equivalent value in return.

Most marketers or corporations miss trade as part of their business and marketing when it comes to selling, or acquiring goods or services, as they have been conditioned to sell and buy for cash. Which is the conventional way. But it does not need to be like this. You can just as easily buy or sell without using any cash by using barter, and it is most probably the easiest, most profitable, and fun way to buy or sell any product or service you may want or need.

In fact, many smart corporations already use barter as their *modus operandi*. The list includes many of the Fortune 100 companies. These corporations have separate trade departments that operate as profit centers. There are also hundreds of trade clubs in the United States. We will be talking extensively about trade clubs in chapter 7.

Barter offers several benefits. First, it saves you money because you are not using it. It is one of the best cash–flow strategies known to financiers. It also allows you to move things you don't need and have already purchased (and are probably depreciating assets) for things that you actually do need and can make you money! Trade allows you to get 100 cents on the dollar for the items that you trade, because trade is always done at full price or "retail."

Having said this, barter or trade is not a "get-rich-quick scheme." It is an honest, legal, and ethical way of doing business. But doing barter trade correctly can certainly make you very wealthy, as it gives you *multiple* times more buying power for the same dollar.

The reason that you may still be a little skeptical about the new world you are about to enter is that you have been trained and conditioned to conduct all your daily commerce and transactions with cash. Anything else would simply not be appropriate. But we are going to teach you a whole new way of doing business that is the reverse of what you are most probably used to and are currently doing. This may take some time and training! But please trust us—it is much more fun and very profitable. Please read this book regularly to maintain your newfound mindset.

For instance, we have been conditioned to think that there are only three types of currency:

- Cash

- Checks

- Credit cards (plastic)

But time, talent, knowledge, expertise, excess, and unused and unsold inventory are also currencies! These can all be traded (bartered) for goods and services you may need, if you know how to package and present your case to a prospective trader.

So, in reality, there are four types of transactions:

- Cash

- Checks

- Credit cards (plastic)

- Barter trade!

And of all the ones listed above, barter trade is the most profitable and a whole lot of fun.

Anything you have that is not being used in your business or life should or could be bartered for something that you can use! This way, you are optimizing all elements of your business and life. Any company of any size can save an immense amount of money by making bartering a part of its portfolio. A large company can easily cut its media expenditures by up to 50 percent by purchasing a portion of its media by bartering its goods and services.

MCHUMOR.com by T. McCracken

"So what if we're in the best preschool?
How can we go anywhere in life if we
don't yet have maxed out credit cards?"

A small company can issue "soft dollars," "funny money," or a "scrip" (which we will be talking about shortly) and trade out its profit, which is one of the easiest barter transactions that you can do. And easily save 25 to 50 percent on its expenditures. You will shortly see real-world examples of how this is done.

With global trade clubs, you could be a dentist in Kalamazoo, Michigan, and use your credit in the club to get a hotel room in Sydney, Australia. You can even put money toward college expenses. Yes, some schools barter their tuition!

All this is possible once you understand trade. Trade is not "smoke and mirrors"; it is a very legitimate and proven alternative way of doing business, and one that is very relevant in today's economy. This is one of the reasons it is used by some of the leading companies in commerce—household names, such as:

- American Express
- NBC
- Levitz
- Hertz
- Sheraton
- Marriott
- Chrysler
- FedEx
- DHL
- Mazda
- KLM

All trade and have been Dave's clients for barter trade, which is one of the primary reasons that they are successful: they are able to leverage their media-buying power. Nearly all major radio and TV stations in the United States trade. Often many of the advertisements that you see in a magazine are paid for with trade dollars, not cash dollars.

FUN FACT

When John Harvard was a young student, his term bills could be paid in produce and livestock.

Although this book is about barter for business, barter is not just about business commerce. It can be used to find a job, keep employees (as an employee-retention strategy), and even find a spouse!

When you are watching TV or listening to a radio station, you are basically seeing the bartering system at its best. The media station trades their content for your time! You implicitly have agreed to allow them to show you their ads and take your time in return for their content. You may not have made the connection. But you have now!

If you are married, you most probably "bartered" your skills, knowledge, education, or personality for a partner!

If you carpool with someone, you are trading your time for theirs.

 **INSIDE SECRET #7**

We all make our livelihood daily by trading something. We just don't make the connection!

If you currently work for someone, you are trading your time for money! Trade is a part of our life and lifestyle.

 # INSIDE SECRET #8

We all barter all the time; it is the way we are programmed. It's part of our DNA. You just don't think about it! Barter trade is an integral part of our life!

As our friend Tony Robbins says,

> "You don't need to have the resources to succeed,
> you just need to be resourceful!"

And the keyword is "resources." You really do have within you the resources to think outside the box. We are all about reframing what is possible when you allow yourself the freedom to think creatively, regardless of the resources available to you.

A lot of the examples that you will see in this book are about people and businesses that had to use barter trade when there was no other alternative available to them. In fact, the first barter trade I did was to make payroll! You will see the full story shortly.

Trading advertising for goods and services certainly works very well, because just like you, the media has unsold goods and services—i.e., airtime.

Now, you may be saying, "I am not a multinational corporation, just an independent professional. How can barter trade help me?" Well, if you are a home-improvement contractor looking for a place to live, how about you find a place that needs some repairs and offer the landlord your repair skills in lieu of rent? You both win. You get a place to live, or a discounted rental, and the land-lord gets his house repaired. If you are a hairstylist, you may trade with someone that owns a restaurant for food. You are only limited by your imagination.

Your arms, legs, voice, talents, etc. can all be traded for something that you may need or want. You can help people move things or buy things that you have a special talent to produce. It all depends on how creative you want to get.

You can also trade your additional hours, excess inventory, or unused services with a radio or media station, either directly or through a trade club, for advertising—the most valued commodity in business—to help gain awareness and get leads. All businesses need advertising. Advertising is the lifeblood of any business. The problem is that most businesses simply don't have the cash to pay for it. But they do have excess time when they are not doing anything. You may be a web designer, graphics designer, copywriter, plumber, painter, gardener, or even a janitorial service. Any media station in the United States can use all of these services.

Many radio stations in the United States trade some of their expenses. It is not uncommon to find them trading landscaping with a local landscape company, or janitorial services with a janitorial person, or tax services with a tax accountant. Because business trade helps lower your expenses and increase your profitability.

Barter really is about being resourceful and seeing opportunities where others see problems. It is no more than having the mindset of getting the most out of whatever you have and being creative about how to put your excess time, talent, inventory, and capital to better use—which in the process gives you immense upside leverage.

INSIDE SECRET #9

The basic concept of barter trade is very simple: you have something that can benefit someone else, and you use this to get what you want rather than paying cash for it. And both parties win in the process.

We hope that reading this book will change your thinking, logic, and beliefs about what is possible, as you will no longer need to think conventionally about how to solve problems.

We believe that the happiest people don't necessarily have the best of everything—they just make the best out of everything they have. Barter will give you that opportunity to make the most out of what you have, be it your time, talent, expertise, or even excess inventory.

Barter, to us, is simply a metaphor for creative thinking. Henry Ford was an out-of-the-box thinker. He developed the assembly line after visiting a slaughterhouse in Chicago, when he saw what was possible. With barter, in the same way, you will become an out-of-the-box thinker. It will allow you to see things and make connections that you have previously not made.

Barter, when done correctly, can be a game changer for your businesses and for your life. Most businesses copy what other businesses do. But by doing this, they can only at best achieve the same results as their competition in terms of growth—and perhaps worse, they end up looking identical to the competition. Just go to the store and notice how many products look identical to each other.

What smart marketers do is simply change the game. They do something new, unique, and novel; they take ideas from other industries. One of the greatest marketers of all time, Steve Jobs, got the idea for the Macintosh computer by studying appliances in Macy's.

If you do something new, you will be able to completely differentiate yourself in the marketplace. When it first came out, an Apple iPhone looked nothing like any other phone, and it performed very differently also. At a time when most people gave away phones, Apple charged a few hundred dollars for a phone that came without a user's manual! It was a product that created its own category.

In the same way, most of your competitors just don't have barter trade on their radar. But you do! You are now looking for every opportunity to trade, and with your newly found barter-trade mindset, you can catapult your business and life to the next level.

Attend any marketing course, and they will tell you that marketing is about finding a need and filling it. Today, the need more than ever is to conserve cash and find creative ways to solve business and life problems. We sincerely hope our book will change the way you view both business and life!

Now that you have been stimulated to think differently about business and life, we can move on.

THINGS TO REMEMBER FROM THIS CHAPTER

- If you don't have money, you invest your time. If you don't have time, you invest your money.

- Barter trade is the oldest form of commerce in the world. You have always known about barter trade; this chapter has just brought it to the surface again. In other words, you are not learning anything new; you're just remembering how to do it again.

- Barter trade does not mean "free." You simply exchange value for value: x = y.

- Barter trade is about being resourceful and creative.

- Barter trade is about people helping people solve every-day problems.

- You have now been stimulated to think differently about what is really possible when you stop reaching for your wallet or checkbook. Welcome to the new universe!

chapter two

— 2 —

Barter?
It's in Our DNA

If you obey the rules, you will miss all of the fun.

Katharine Hepburn

To be an effective trader, you need to shift your mindset from conventional to creative. Barter is all about *not* following conventional rules—i.e., using cash, checks, or credit cards to acquire goods and services. It is about being different and creative, and trading your goods and services instead of using conventional cash or checks. And when you learn to do it right, it is very profitable and a whole lot of fun!

It is very profitable because what you barter or use for trade is usually an idle or underutilized asset. It could be an empty room in your house, rooms in your hotel, excess inventory, products, goods, or services.

Something is better than nothing!

Barter provides you with a very unique opportunity to convert idle assets into something very useful to you: goods and services that you need and can obtain without paying cash.

If what you trade is unsold product or service, or extra time, whatever you gain in return is your new "unfound wealth." It's something that you really got for nothing—or maybe even for free?

At midnight every night, millions of dollars of products, services,

---

FUN FACT

In 1922, Thomas Edison proposed an experiment in the United States with a commodity dollar of constant purchasing power backed by goods. It never caught on.

---

and airtime literally evaporate into thin air, because they were unused or not sold. And anyone would rather trade with you rather than lose what they have; that is just good business sense. This is the concept behind standby seats offered on flights.

If you are looking to trade for food, it is best to approach a grocery store that has inventory it has not been able to sell and is going to expire in twenty-four hours. They will be very predispositioned to trade with you for whatever you have! Again, something is better than nothing.

I have been able to get Super Bowl time for about twenty cents on the dollar. No, that is not a typo—twenty cents on the dollar. Why? Because the networks were not able to sell them at full rack or retail rate. And they would rather sell it off at what they can get instead of letting it go. Again, it is just good business sense. I was then able to turn around and sell this time at huge markups, while paying pennies on the dollar. As the broker, I was able to make a significant amount of money for myself doing this.

How can this be possible?

 # INSIDE SECRET #10

In the world of barter, something is better than nothing. As the clock approaches midnight, more people will want to trade with you before what they have evaporates into thin air!

Let me give you another simple example to help drive this very important point home. All businesses in the world have times when they have nothing to do but still have sunk or invested capital.

A printing company may have two hours per day that their machines are running idle. But they already have paid for all the fixed overhead, insurance, rents, payroll, and utilities that go into running their operation.

If they were smart, they could trade this unused spare time with a local media station for advertising to help promote their business in the local area. All media stations need printing work done: flyers, newsletters, brochures, etc. So the media gets the printing it needs, and the printing company gets much-needed advertising to grow its business in tough times. All by using their excess, idle time and capacity.

In this example, which actually is a real example, you see the power of barter trade in action. Both parties paid for the valuable goods or services they needed using their excess time or inventory. In barter trade, everyone wins, and there is no catch!

The printing company's expensive printing press was sitting idle for two hours a day. The local media station had unsold time. They traded, and both businesses grew and benefitted.

INSIDE SECRET #11

In barter, both sides win. Although people try to find the catch, there is none!

Yes, the printing company may have used ink and paper that it may not have normally used if their equipment was lying idle. And they could charge the media company a service charge for this. But at the end of the day, you end up with a very powerful, lucrative transaction for both parties.

The printing company would have the same rights and privileges for airtime as if it were paying cash, and vice versa for the media company.

INSIDE SECRET #12

A barter deal is identical to a cash deal. The only difference is that you don't pay with cash!

We are now about to let you into another secret that most amateurs who get into barter trade forget. And that is:

INSIDE SECRET #13

Barter is not designed to replace any cash transactions that you are currently doing; it is meant to supplement them—i.e., add to them.

If you can sell what you have for cash, you don't need barter trade. But if you cannot sell what you have for cash, barter provides an ideal medium to sell it for trade.

 **INSIDE SECRET #14**

Barter trade is simply a tool to use to provide you with leverage—i.e., maximum impact with minimal effort.

With all the benefits that barter trade has, it always makes sense to seek barter opportunities whenever possible. We both would rather barter than pay cash for goods and services, because barter yields immense benefits, which you are about to learn. But we do live in a "cash world," and not everyone understands the benefits of barter. Hence we wrote this book.

However, when people have products or services that they cannot sell for cash or that are approaching midnight (i.e., about to expire), they will be very interested in trading with you.

WHAT IS BARTER?

Barter, by definition, is the legal exchange of goods and services in a mutually beneficial manner. You trade something that you have for something you usually need and want, and both parties benefit in the process. It is a "cashless" process. No cash changes hands.

 **INSIDE SECRET #15**

In true orthodox barter trade, it would be illegal to exchange cash!

Barter is also used by nations, and this practice is called "counter trade," an accepted way to make trading more convenient for nations that have difficulty with currency conversion, as well as

MᴄHUMOR.ᴄᴏᴍ by T. McCracken

"Apparently your DNA is composed of
battery acids instead of nucleic acids."

for nations with fewer financial resources but sufficient commodities. For example, a country that produces plenty of rice may exchange it with another nation to acquire another type of grain, or fruits and vegetables. On the other hand, one country might trade foodstuffs for textiles or oil.

WHY BARTER?

You have already seen a few limited examples of how to use barter. Listed below are some other reasons you may want to look into barter trade, as it:

- Improves your margins

- Optimizes your resources

- Allows you to build new sales channels

- Saves you cash that stays in your pocket!

- Allows you to set up a bank in a matter of seconds

- Is the best loyalty program you can have, hands down!

- Can create buying and purchasing power for you at will

- Give you higher multiples of buying power of at least three to five times!

- Allows you to pay at steep discounts, with no interest

- Explodes your response rate for direct mailings

- Allows you to conserve cash, as you don't use it

- Allows you to create your own currency or "scrip"

- Works the opposite as cash: you actually get rewarded the longer you take to pay

At bare minimum, with a trade deal you get what you want right now, you end up buying at a steep discount, and you pay for it at some time in the future at a zero-percent interest rate. You really can't go wrong!

A very famous marketing consultant for several years had all of his house decorating, furniture purchases, and house painting done through barter. He would give to someone and he would get in return the same value for their service. He was even able to get his wife a brand-new Porsche convertible for just a day and a half of his time! He clearly understands the dynamics of barter trade. And all the benefits of barter listed above. We hope you are now starting to see the power of barter trade.

We live with the mindset that the only form of currency that exists is a dollar-based one. And that we can only obtain goods and services by paying for them with cash, checks, or credit cards. Not true! If I obtain $100 worth of goods from you, I don't need to give you a $100 bill. I could just as easily trade you products or services that I own, that only cost me $25. This saves me $75, but it still gives you $100 worth of value. This is the essence of barter!

But the real reason that you may want to consider barter trade lies in your answer to the following question: Would you rather write a check, or use something that you already have in your possession and have paid for?

NO CASH REQUIRED! PLEASE KEEP YOUR WALLET IN YOUR DRAWER

Throughout my (Dave's) forty-plus years in barter trade, whenever I have talked to a client about a potential barter-trade deal, the first thing I tell them is to leave their wallet in the drawer. I don't want any money from them. This usually results in them looking at me like a man from Mars! It really is a paradigm shift for them.

Barter takes time, it takes education, but the payoff is big!

When I moved down to Florida, I needed a dry cleaner, and I met a dry cleaner that was just about to open business. I proposed a trade. I would advertise his business extensively for two days at forty-eight times per day, or twice per hour in thirty-second commercials—in return for free dry cleaning for life. Yes, *free* dry cleaning for life! He agreed!

The offer I put over the air for him was free dry cleaning if you brought your clothes in over the next two days only. As many items as you wanted!

I explained to the dry cleaner a concept that Ali talks about in his book *Get Your Black Belt in Marketing*, which is the "lifetime value of a customer"—i.e., how much a customer is worth to you over the lifetime they do business with you. Think long term, not short term. A percentage of people who would take him up on this offer will stay for life and become long-term, cash-paying customers.

The advertising I ran over two days brought in four hundred people, and 50 percent of those are still customers today, five years later! The two hundred customers he acquired through the campaign helped him stay in business to this very day. In barter trade, both sides win.

Here again you see in a very simple example how the power of barter trade results in a win-win situation. The dry cleaner got the advertising it needed to do a grand opening!

The lifetime value of a customer is one of the most powerful but misunderstood marketing techniques. It can easily be used to double or triple your sales. The million-dollar question in marketing Ali's clients ask him is, "How much should I be spending on my marketing?" Ali's response is, "It depends on how much your customers are making you."

If you are a chiropractor and you charge $200 per visit, and each customer that you acquire on average visits you 3 times a year for 5 years, and on average refers 3 people, of which one becomes a paying client also, then your total lifetime revenue from each customer is:

3 customer visits x $200 = $600 x 5 years = $3,000

1 referral client @ $200 x 3 = $600 x 5 years = $3,000

Total revenue = $6,000 (not $200 for one visit!)

Your marketing budget can now be calculated based on the total revenue a single customer may generate over their lifetime. As Ali points out, marketing is a simple math problem.

In the above simple example, you could easily provide $500 to your lead source, as each customer is generating $6,000 for you over the lifetime of doing business with you.

ONLY BARTER CAN GIVE YOU 100 PERCENT RETURN ON YOUR ADVERTISING

If you are an independent professional or a small business, you are already spending money on advertising. Maybe at the low end you spend $1,000 per month on ads in the yellow pages. If you are a medium-sized business, you may spend $10,000 to $20,000 in ads in major trade magazines to generate leads.

But what if we changed our thinking for a second, as this book is all about thinking differently. What if the small local business started to issue or print its own currency or voucher (what barter experts call a "scrip," which we will be talking extensively about shortly)—and either traded this with a local media station or just gave it out to the local community?

Well, you could issue twice as many vouchers as the current $1,000 per month. This immediately doubles your advertising spend, or purchasing power.

Next, you could trade your vouchers with a local newspaper, radio station, or other media. The media would give you airtime or print space in return.

Now remember, since you are paying in vouchers, the vouchers can only be redeemed at your place of business. This means that whoever uses the voucher must use it at your place of business for it to be valid. This is what we call in trade "recycled advertising." Your advertising dollars just went back into your pocket. You get a 100-percent return on your advertising. This is better than pay-per-click advertising, because in pay-per-click advertising (like Google's), you are only paying for a lead. Pay per click is simply pay per lead. Here you are paying for a sale! Big difference! You're only paying for the portion of advertising that generates results, or what we in marketing called "results-based advertising," or "pay-per-sale advertising." Is that not the way that advertising should be? This way every dollar you spend on advertising is coming straight back into your business. This is the power of barter trade. You will shortly see how the City of Palm Springs in Florida used this exact strategy to promote the city across the United States.

THE TWO RS OF BARTER TRADE

Barter trade is really about reusing assets that you have already invested in and recycling them into something of use, and getting out of the habit of reaching for your wallet, checkbook, or checkcard. To make barter trade work, you just need to follow a few simple rules.

- Find out what you have to trade.
- Find out who needs what you have to offer.

Barter is all about the two Rs: Reusing and Recycling assets.

BARTER VERSUS CASH

But if barter is older than cash and so much more profitable, how and why did we evolve to a cash-based economy? Maybe a short lesson in monetary economics may help before we dive deeper into the mechanics of barter. Before money existed as we know it, people traded goods directly, and then later commodities, to get what they wanted. Very early on, precious metals became the foremost commodity-based forms of payment. Various metals would have different prescribed levels of importance: copper would have its own value, as would silver and gold. Presumably these coins had intrinsic value and could be melted down or sold as necessary.

History tells us that the use of precious metals then led to coinage. The Lydians, located in modern Turkey, are credited with producing the first stamped coins in 650 BC, and experts suggest that contemporary Ionians and Greeks used similar types of coins. And the Babylonians are credited with developing the precursor to the modern-day economic system.

But the British pound sterling is credited as the first "legal tender." It was developed in the late seventeenth century, backed by a promise to the carrier that they were redeemable for gold upon the bearer's request. A one-pound note was therefore redeemable for one troy ounce of gold.

This led to what we know as the beginning of the "gold standard," in which the notes in circulation did not exceed the gold in reserves. The strength of the currency relied on the fact that notes could be exchanged at a bank by the bearer—or that they were, as the saying goes, as good as gold!

The period from 1880 to 1914 was known as the classical gold standard period. During that time, the majority of countries adhered to the gold standard.

FUN FACT

The saying "It is as good as gold" came from the fact that gold was used to back currencies, which were promissory notes or IOUs. Up to that time, people had used precious metals, gold or silver, and they had real intrinsic value.

Gold certificates were used in the United States from 1882 to 1933 as a form of paper currency. Each certificate gave its holder title to its corresponding amount of gold coin. Therefore, this type of paper currency was intended to represent actual gold coin-

FUN FACT

On August 15, 1971, the United States defaulted on its promise to pay gold for dollars.

age. In 1933, the practice of redeeming these notes for gold coins was ended by the United States government.

IN GOD WE TRUST, BECAUSE OUR CURRENCY IS NOT BACKED UP BY ANY GOLD!

The cash economy we operate in today only works because we *believe* that a dollar is worth a "real" dollar, when it is in fact a promise to pay nothing! It really is an illusion! Our current currency is backed up by nothing. Today we have basically created our own economy based on faith, and use cash simply as paper to represent our trust.

Compare this to our ancestors' barter economy. A barter economy is more stable and economically sound, because the goods and services that stand behind what you are offering are both tangible and real, and thus your promise to pay is much more robust and real.

Fort Knox is supposed to be our gold reserve. This is a United

FUN FACT

The website of the US Mint says that the 147.3 million troy ounces of gold in Fort Knox are held as an asset of the United States.

States Army post in Kentucky, south of Louisville and north of Elizabethtown. The amount of gold held in Fort Knox is said to have reached 701 million ounces around 1949 (per Wikipedia). At one time, the United States was said to have had about 69.9 percent of all the gold in the world!

So now you know why it says "In God We Trust" on our legal tender: our currency is not backed by any gold!

THE EMERGENCE OF A NEW ECONOMY: BARTER IS REBORN IN 1929

Modern-day commerce started with barter trade, and it then moved to coins and cash somewhere around the late seventeenth century. But what most people don't know is that:

 **INSIDE SECRET #16**

Barter was reborn around 1929 and was big with the media in the 1950s.

What was so important about 1929? And how did this help the rebirth of barter trade? This was the Great Depression, and people did not have cash. And when cash is short, people get very creative and figure out how they can get the same thing without using any cash. No cash, no problem! Savvy business people during the Great Depression of the late 1920s quickly figured out that barter was a very powerful financial instrument—and could be used to solve their cash-flow problems.

In the late 1940s, after the World War II, we had another depression. This time the media figured out how great barter was as a leverage tool, and they started to heavily trade their excess capacity with businesses.

In the Great Depression of 1929, many businesses could not pay their bills, and so was born the most powerful weapon in barter

---

FUN FACT

Historically, when times get tough, you see a 50-percent-plus increase in bartering as a way for people to be able to buy things or get things, and do it economically. - C. Britt Beemer, chairman of America's Research Group

---

trade business: a "scrip" or "due bill." Creditors turned up at the business establishment and would say: "The bill is due, and I understand that you can't pay. I am going to eat here (or use your services), and you can write the amount in your ledger."

A due bill or scrip is simply a voucher that can be used as a form of payment. Even today due bills are well understood in the financial community. They are defined as a financial instrument used to document and identify the seller's obligation to deliver securities sold to the buyer.

 **INSIDE SECRET #17**

The most powerful weapon in a barter trader's toolbox is the power to issue a scrip at any time.

So a scrip is no more than a sophisticated gift voucher, only redeemable at your place of business. When those businesses in the Great Depression could not pay their bills, they would simply issue a scrip to the value of the credit—i.e., a restaurant would issue a scrip of $1,000 of food at its restaurant if it owed someone $1,000 worth of products or services.

This concept worked so well that barter was reborn and scrip became the universal currency for barter professionals, and it continues to this very day.

In fact, you see scrips every day but do not recognize them. When you get a gift card to Target or Sears, these are simply scrips: vouchers that are only redeemable at their business establishment. We owe thanks to the barter industry that we have so-called gift cards, as gift cards started their life as due bills.

The only difference from a gift voucher as you may know it is that a scrip used by a barter professional has specific terms and conditions for its use.

Below is an example of a real scrip, issued by a restaurant in Florida, to help you see what we mean.

Yes, you can issue your own currency! And set whatever terms and conditions you like.

Due Bill Conditions

1.) Due bill good for food, beverage and tax.
2.) Tips must be paid in cash.
3.) Due bill has no cash value.
4.) Due bill good to the nearest dollar: no change given.

FOOD & BEVERAGE CERTIFICATE

$10.00 $10.00

This certificate is good for $10.00 in food,
Beverage & tax. See other side for conditions

Expiration Date: _____   _____

$10.00 $10.00

As a merchant or business, you can ethically and legally create a scrip or voucher and use this just like cash to pay vendors and acquire the products and services you need. Your credit is just as good as that issued by the US Government. In fact, maybe better—because you or your business stands behind it! As the old saying goes, "You are as good as your word."

So you legally can issue a scrip for your business as shown above. All you need to do is to understand that

A GIFT VOUCHER = A VOUCHER = A FORM OF PAYMENT

And you must honor the credit!

So instead of giving you $500 worth of food, I could just as easily give you a $500 gift voucher or scrip for my restaurant in which I set specific terms and conditions of use, as outlined in the scrip above:

- Expiration date

- How the tips must be paid

- What is covered

- How change would be handled

 # INSIDE SECRET #18

To become a true barter master, you will need to master the concept of barter scrip. This is at the heart of all the deals you will be doing.

Sounds simple? It is! But it is also extremely powerful, because creating your own currency will give you a tremendous amount of leverage, flexibility, and, of course, responsibility! You have now just created a bank and have started printing your own currency—all legally, of course. It is legal tender that is only redeemable at your place of business and backed by your product or services. But you must make good on your promises!

 # INSIDE SECRET #19

Scrip is often referred to as funny money!

Barter masters call scrip "funny money" to differentiate it from what we know as "real money." You will also often see people refer to scrip as soft currency, which is very similar to the concept of "paper" or "notes" used in the world of real estate. If an owner of a property sells his or her house, they can issue a note that makes them the bank and determine their payment terms. This is called "carrying the paper" in the real estate world.

In the same way, by issuing your own currency, you become a bank. And by standing behind your offering, you can legally start issuing your own currency, redeemable at your place of business, that can give you multiple advantages that only barter masters understand.

 # INSIDE SECRET #20

You don't need to break the bank. Just understand breakage!

The emergence of scrip around 1929 created a very unique bartering tool, because it provided unmatched flexibility—as all the scrip is not (and is often not) all used.

For example, if I am a restaurant owner, I could issue you a scrip for $500 worth of food at my restaurant in five pieces of paper worth $100, which would basically be IOUs for my goods and services that you can use as you please over the time period specified on the scrip.

But what happens if you come to my restaurant and eat $200 worth of food, and then lose or never use the $300 worth of vouchers that you have left within the expiration period? This unused portion of your scrip or trade is called "breakage."

What barter experts have found over the decades is that on average only 80 percent of a scrip will ever be redeemed. On average, there is significant breakage. But what happens to the unused portion of the scrip, the portion you don't use or that even expires? It comes straight back to the bottom line.

How often have you left thirty cents, fifty cents, or maybe a dollar on a gift card? This is the breakage, or the unused portion of the voucher or scrip.

A few cents on every gift card adds up to several million dollars in breakage that goes straight back to the bottom line of the person that issued it.

Now before you start to think that barter is being manipulative or unethical, we need to point out that:

INSIDE SECRET #21

It is a truism that people will almost never redeem 100 percent of a barter scrip. Nothing to do with barter trade; it's just human nature.

Breakage is a very powerful concept that few people understand, unless you have been trained in barter economics. It is so powerful that it is used as SOP, or standard operating procedure, for many businesses that factor it into their revenue model. All airlines, for example, budget for people who will not show up for a flight—this is why you have flights that are oversold. They turned up, and breakage worked against them!

Now that you understand breakage, we can introduce another term, which is called "dating." This dating doesn't have to do with falling in love, but the time period the scrip was issued for.

INSIDE SECRET #22

The duration of the scrip is called dating.

Once we are able to both issue a scrip and put a date of redemption on it, or "dating," we have in essence created a very powerful tool, because:

INSIDE SECRET #23

The longer the dating you give someone, the higher the breakage is likely to be!

Herein lies a very important point:

BARTER TRADE WORKS THE OPPOSITE AS CASH!

If I offer you a scrip for $500 for products or services only valued for two days, you would most likely bring in your whole family and all your friends the next day to take advantage of the scrip before you lose it. But if I made the dating five years, you would likely spread out your consumption over a few years, and probably not use all of the scrip.

So breakage works the opposite as cash: the longer I make my scrip or voucher or IOU valid, the less likely it will all be redeemed. Or, the longer the scrip, the less I end up paying—unlike the cash world, where if you borrow from the bank, the longer the term of your loan, the more you end up paying in interest and charges.

The concept of breakage is something that retailers understand very well, and it works to their advantage. It has been estimated that anywhere between 10 to 20 percent of all gift vouchers or cards are not redeemed, amounting to a gain for retailers of about $8 billion in the United States in 2006.

Breakage is used by insurance companies' actuaries and is actually built into their calculations.

Many smart traders will bet and bank on the breakage—i.e., that a portion of the scrip is not going to be redeemed. Aggressive barter traders simply budget a breakage amount into any deal that they do. I have known people budget up to a 90-percent breakage rate! Yes, 90 percent of the scrip goes unused! A few real-world case studies may help you understand the power of breakage.

Maybe you are too young to remember the famous S&H Green Stamps known as Green Shield Stamps. They were very popular in the United States from the 1930s until the late 1980s. They were distributed as part of a rewards program operated by the Sperry and Hutchinson Company (S&H), founded in 1896.

During the 1960s, the rewards catalog printed by the company was the largest publication in the United States, and the company issued three times as many stamps as the US Postal Service! Customers would receive stamps at the checkout counter of supermarkets, department stores, gasoline stations, and other retailers, which could be redeemed for products in the catalog. Consumers got $1.20 in value for every 1,200 green stamps they collected.

Ali's mum brought their first electric kettle using Green Shield Stamps!

Now here is the lesson in breakage that S&H understood very well and budgeted into their *modus operandi* for the business: 97 percent of the people never came back! Only 3 percent of stamps were redeemed! If they were all redeemed, the company would have gone bankrupt a long time ago!

But you need to be very careful with breakage, and be an expert trader, before you start factoring breakage into your transactions. You should test and get to know your numbers first.

But once you figure out your breakage, it can really do amazing things for your business.

HOW TO USE BREAKAGE TO GET $125,000 WORTH OF FREE ADVERTISING—AND EVEN $3,000 FOR A HOLIDAY!

A good case study for us to share with you to show the incredible impact of breakage is one of the very first barter deals I did. I owned a radio station in New Orleans and traded advertising on fifty radio stations across the United States for rooms in a New Orleans hotel.

I traded $125,000 worth of radio and TV advertising time by giving them barter scrip in that amount with a one-year expiration date. In return, they gave me the equivalent in rooms.

The hotel immediately got $125,000 in advertising that it had been paying $125,000 for in real cash. But it got it on trade or barter now by trading for the equivalent amount in rooms that were basically empty.

At the end of twelve months, an audit revealed that only $35,000 worth of the barter scrip had been redeemed within the time-limit period. The hotel had 100 rooms, but we had only used 28 rooms, or 28 percent of the total value of the script ($35,000 out of $125,000). The breakage on the script was *72 percent. This was not planned but is what actually happened!* The rest expired and went unused. The cash cost of the hotel delivering $35,000 worth of rooms was only $5,000 in hard cash.

MCHUMOR.com by T. McCracken

"Try to think of bankruptcy
as an accounting procedure."

So, in essence, the hotel had leveraged up $125,000 in advertising on trade with "soft dollars" or "funny money" for 5,000 hard dollars.

However, that did not take into consideration two overlooked (but extremely significant) other factors.

- Statistically, $35,000 in room trade produces $17,500 in food, beverage, and miscellaneous "cash" sales with a gross profit in excess of $8,000 for the hotel. Hotels make a very healthy margin on the incidentals! The incidentals were nearly 50 percent of additional revenue, not part of the scrip! This is what we call the "upsell" in marketing.

- Now if you stop and think about what happened here, the hotel actually got paid $3,000 net after all costs to enter into the trade ($8,000 profit from the food, beverages, etc., less $5,000 hard cost to fulfill the $35,000 worth of rooms).

- Also, all of the $35,000 worth of rooms were not used at one time. Usage was spread out over twelve months—meaning that the hotel got to pay the $5,000 over twelve months totally interest free.

But when all the dust settled, *they got $125,000 worth of free advertising and $3,000 for a holiday!*

Once they entered into a barter-trade deal with me, they cut their cash advertising by essentially trading empty rooms for media time, and once the incidentals were factored in, they actually made $3,000 in cash!

Now before you ask how much it costs the radio station to run $125,000 worth of advertising—the answer is $0. If a radio station is making a profit (which most are), anything they sell is simply pure profit, as it is unused time that they were not able to sell using cash.

So here again you see how barter is a win-win.

FLOAT BECOMES YOUR SHORT-TERM INVESTMENTS IN BARTER

Now you understand the key barter instruments: scrip, breakage, and dating. This leads to the final barter concept, called "float."

INSIDE SECRET #24

A float is the money you have access to during the dating period.

In conventional romance, dating is expensive, but in the world of barter, the longer the dating, the more chance you have of breakage (i.e., the scrip not being used), and at the same time, you have access to the money during the period of the dating! Both of these elements compound to yield a very profitable transaction.

If I issue you a scrip for $10,000 with a five-year dating, until you use any portion of the scrip, I still have the money in my bank. The amount I have in the bank is called the float.

But why is float so important in the barter world? Because float allows you to take the money that is sitting idle and put it into short-term securities. Understanding this very simple principal has made American Express one of the most famous and powerful financial institutions in the world!

American Express issues travelers checks, which are basically scrip—because as you know now, scrip is simply a voucher or IOU. But most people don't use the travelers' checks straight away, and some may never use them at all! Yes, breakage! And until they are redeemed, American Express has the float, or use of the funds, and can put the money into short-term securities. American Express makes several millions of dollars on scrip for travelers' checks, since in some cases they have use of the funds for nine months!

Let's recap to make sure you got it.

As you have seen, we started with a very simple concept of replacing your cash transaction with a trade transaction: no need for your wallet, cash, or credit card. The cashless transaction came back into fashion around 1929—but more out of necessity, because of the Great Depression and businesses' inability to pay their bills. But what resulted was the birth of the most powerful financial instrument in our history: the scrip, or voucher, or IOU. Barter experts then realized that a scrip could be used creatively, and this in turn led to the concepts of breakage, dating, and floats. All of these, when used intelligently, can lead to significant cash-generating opportunities, as you have seen.

 # INSIDE SECRET #25

To become a true barter expert, you need to understand and feel very comfortable with the four pillars of barter: scrip, dating, breakage, and float. These are the four foundational pillars on which all barter trade is built. Master these and you will be among the top 1 percent of financiers in the world.

THINGS TO REMEMBER FROM THIS CHAPTER

- Barter trade is all about moving from conventional to creative thinking.

- We are so entrenched in the dollar-based cash and credit system that we forget there is a whole new way to do commerce called barter trade, which is perfectly legal and was previously used prior to cash.

- Everyone wins in barter, and there is no catch.

- Barter works with cash; it is a vehicle to both conserve and generate it.

- Barter is the best way to recycle your advertising dollars back into your business.

- You can issue your own legal currency. This is called a scrip, or funny money (as opposed to "real money").

- Scrip, dating, breakage, and floats create immense leverage opportunities. They are the four pillars of barter trade.

chapter three
—— 3 ——
The 7 Myths of Barter Dispelled

Fools ignore complexity. Pragmatists suffer it.
Some can avoid it. Geniuses simply remove it.

Alan Perlis

One of our favorite shows is *MythBusters*, a show that basically removes the myths surrounding a certain concept. In this chapter, we are going to try to dispel the myths surrounding barter trade, give you a clear and objective overview of barter trade, and explain why we think it needs to be part of your business or personal portfolio.

We believe that barter trade is probably one of the most misunderstood concepts in the business world, because we have forgotten how to trade and are so deeply entrenched in a cash- and plastic/credit card–based economy. But when done correctly, barter always provides a win-win situation, or a mutually beneficial outcome, for all parties involved. Anyone can barter trade, as we all have either excess time or unused, unwanted, and underleveraged products or services.

We understand that a lot of you may still be skeptical, because you are still in the linear-thinking mindset.

INSIDE SECRET #26

Barter trade is not for the fainthearted or the linear thinkers; it requires you to step out of your comfort zone and into your creative zone.

If barter is so good, then why are more people not using this as part of their everyday life and business? As we said before, we think the primary reason for this is lack of education. And as you will see throughout this book, barter really is an art. Yes, it takes longer than a straight cash transaction to negotiate the terms of the deal. It is just like creating an art masterpiece, but it is a lot more fun and immensely lucrative, if you understand it and do it correctly—as you have seen in some of the examples we have already shown you. And there are a lot more to come!

We have found:

INSIDE SECRET #27

The biggest reason more people and businesses don't trade is that they simply don't know how to! They lack the education and know-how about what barter really is and how it really works!

Most people think that barter trade does not even exist today. We are happy to tell you that barter trade is alive, vibrant, and very strong.

There are literally hundreds of trade clubs across the United States that trade millions of dollars daily. The local trade club in Silicon Valley, where Ali lives, trades about $5,000,000 per year, and that is just one office in one city in the United States. Its members include every imaginable service and product you can think of, with about 1,500 total members.

McHUMOR.com by T. McCracken

"I swear to tell the truth, the whole truth and nothing but the truth ... almost."

Lack of awareness, knowledge, and education is certainly a key reason why more people don't use trade as a form of commerce. But besides this, there are also some other reasons that we call the "7 Killer Myths of Barter Trade." They are:

MYTH 1: ONLY POOR PEOPLE BARTER OR TRADE.

We hope by now you are convinced that trade is not just for "poor people" but for all people—especially smart people! You have seen numerous examples of how it can give you immense leverage very quickly. You can start today and trade for as much as you can fulfill. So trade gives you unlimited purchasing power. No other marketing tool can give you the leverage that barter can.

If you have something that you no longer need or use, it makes more sense to trade it for something you may need or want.

In the short case studies that are to follow, you will clearly see how I traded what most people would call trash, and recycled this "trash" into treasure that made a lot of money for me and the people I put the deals together for! And you can do the same, once you get the trade mindset.

If you think only poor people trade, think again. Trade is the new currency of the twenty-first century!

MYTH 2: WHY TRADE, WHEN IT IS JUST AS EASY TO SELL?

If you can sell your product or service for cash, that is good, and we certainly do not want to stop you. But if you are able to find someone that will trade with you rather than take cash, you would be better off trading. This way you are conserving cash by not using it, while at the same time leveraging your buying spend. And if you cannot sell what you have for cash, then barter is an ideal alternative or vehicle for you.

Yes, cash allows for instantaneous transactions, and cash is both convenient and universal. But when cash is short, it is actually easier to trade, and barter trade always flourishes in down economies.

Yes, barter trade takes education and patience, but it is a very profitable and lucrative profession when done right, because you can take old, unused products or services, or excess time or capacity that you have paid for, and now monetize these at full market value, as opposed to the conventional way of getting rid of excess inventory by liquidation "closeout" or "fire sales." Using barter trade, you end up getting full retail value. Barter eliminates the need for discounting. You will see real-world case studies shortly.

MYTH 3: NOBODY WILL TRADE WITH ME.

Do you remember when you were in high school? Did you trade playing cards or something with your friends? Maybe your lunch or some games? Remember, you could always find someone to trade with, right? In the same way, we promise you that you can always find someone to do a barter trade deal with you today; it's a skill you have built into your DNA!

Mutant Jeans

To trade, you basically have two options. You can put what you have or want to trade into a trade club. There are both local and national barter trade clubs all over the United States.

Trade clubs eliminate the need to find people who think like you and like to do business like you—i.e., prefer to trade instead of pay cash! In these clubs, you will find some of the smartest business people in the world! And some very successful businesses also. Nearly all the major media in the United States are members of some trade club. Club membership also includes major hotel chains, major league football franchises, other major franchises, etc.

 INSIDE SECRET #28

You would be very surprised to see who is "in the club" and would immediately recognize them. They are all household names and people you would know or like to trade with.

For confidentiality reasons, we cannot publish the names of people who are members of trade clubs. But once you join, you will have immediate access to these folks and understand what we mean.

Nearly every type of product or service imaginable is part of a trade club. And trade clubs are associated with other trade clubs around the world, which means if you are a dentist and join a respectable trade club in Walnut Creek, California, you could do some work for a lawyer in San Francisco, California. The lawyer's account is debited and your account is credited with the equivalent "funny money" or barter credits, and now you have x barter trade bucks to spend with anyone in the club! So the dental work you did for the lawyer in San Francisco could get you credits for a hotel room in Sydney, Australia. The trade club accounting system would handle the accounting, processing, etc.

So now you are seeing how trade clubs work. It is simply like-minded people working together in a controlled marketing environment. It is a network of people who trade with each other, with the club keeping the records. Each gains equivalent value, and it eliminates the need to try to find people who have the "barter-trade" mindset. You simply become part of the club! A full list of trade clubs or barter exchanges may be found at nate.org or irta.com. Before you join an exchange, ask if they will show you a directory of its members. This will give you an idea of people who you can do business with. Trust us, you will be surprised; this is one of the major secrets of the world's top barter traders.

Once you join a trade club, you will be assigned an account rep. This person will ask you to fill out a profile of your business, product, and service, and they will market this to other members of the club. It is just like adding another sales representative to your company, but at no additional cost! You also have a captive audience of people already willing to trade with you (i.e., members of the club).

 **INSIDE SECRET #29**

One of the other key advantages of joining a trade club is that it acts as a marketing organization for you, helping you sell your product or service to other members!

So trade clubs are your answer to finding like-minded people— those business people and individuals who understand the leverage opportunity that trade offers and want to preserve their cash. And do business the smart way.

You don't need to be a business to join a trade club; you can also be an individual who has something to trade, some product or service that would be valuable to other members of the community.

There is usually a small monthly fee to join this type of club, and they take a small percentage of the transaction, but in return you become part of an exclusive club or network of people that truly understands the benefits of barter trade.

But I Wanna Go It Alone!

Trade clubs are basically marketing brokers: they broker transactions, and this is the way they make money. They are ideal for people who are new to barter trade and for people who cannot find people to trade with. Certainly there is nothing to stop you from going direct and setting up your own barter-trade deals, and we encourage you to do this. But trade clubs are a perfect place to "cut your teeth" first, and we highly recommend you start here.

Also, if you go it alone, you may still run into another problem. How do you approach the whole business of trade?

If you are a plumber who walked into Walmart today and told the cashier that you wanted to pay for your $1,000 worth of purchases with ten hours' worth of plumbing time, you most probably would be escorted by security out of the store!

But the promise of this book is "No Cash? No Problem!" How do we get around this?

 **INSIDE SECRET #30**

Rule #1 of barter trade is to only deal with the principal who writes the checks and has the authority to make decisions.

When I (Ali) went to meet Dave down in Florida, I took him some homemade chicken pie, because a few weeks earlier he had been to my house in San Francisco, and he had loved the chicken pie that my wife had made for him.

I hand-carried the homemade pie my wife had made from San Francisco, California, to Florida, a full-day's trip starting at 4:00 a.m., and gave it to Dave in Starbucks late that evening in Tampa, where we met that night to discuss this book.

On the way out of Starbucks, Dave asked one of the servers, "Would you give me a cup of coffee, if I give you a chicken pie?" She smiled and politely said no!

I was amazed—why would Dave offer the chicken pie that I had painstakingly brought across the United States? So I asked Dave, "Why did you offer her the chicken pie?" His response: "To teach you the most important lesson in barter!"

I asked him what this might be. His response?

 # INSIDE SECRET #31

"You can only barter with a person that is in a position to barter."

He went on to explain that the server at the Starbucks had no interest in saving the company money or doing barter deals—just getting a paycheck. But the owner of the franchise gets up every day with just one thing on his or her mind, and that is how to make or save money.

So if we had got to the owner of the business and had shown them how to make or save money, we most probably could have done a trade. Okay, I agree, they may not really want a chicken pie, but Dave drove the point home to me, that I just had to find the decision maker. It was worth my trip to Florida just to learn this.

Why is this lesson so important to you? Because if you called a media station and asked them if they would barter with you directly for your goods and services, the answer would be no! And you would think that everything that you are being taught in this book is wrong.

The truth is all media stations trade, and:

INSIDE SECRET #32

The only person in a media company that really knows how much business is done through trade and how much is done through conventional cash is the CEO or the owner—no one else!

So although you may be told by the person who picks up the phone that the media station does not barter, the reality is that it does. And this is the secret that only five hundred people around the world know. All the media in the United States and the world will trade—that is, if you know how to go about it and get to the right person (the chicken pie lesson).

I (Dave) have been in the business for forty years and know many of the media folks across the United States. They also know me, and they trust that I will do good, ethical barter trade with them.

In your case, again, it is best to start by joining a local trade club, which major media are a part of, and then trade with them, so they get to know you, like you, and trust you. The media will only trade with you directly if they trust that you are a person of integrity and are known in the field. No different than a cash business, large corporations only want to do business with proven entities.

Now you may be asking, why does the media not simply let people know that they would like to trade with you? The reason for this is, as we explained before, barter is not supposed to replace cash transactions, only supplement them. The media or any business does not want to cannibalize its existing cash business for trade business. Trade was introduced as simply a tool to gain leverage. I created radio barter out of necessity, as I needed to pay my bills and just did not have the cash!

INSIDE SECRET #33

It is true that cash is king, as cash is universal and can be used instantaneously. But barter is a great tool to get it!

Barter, as we pointed out earlier, was reborn out of necessity. Remember when we talked about the Great Depression of 1929 and how this led to the emergence of scrip as a new financial instrument? This was the rebirth of barter trade as we know it. In the same way, after World War II, businesses and the media had excess capacity that they could not sell for cash, and so they decided to trade for it.

INSIDE SECRET #34

Barter will always flourish in a down economy!

Barter, when it came back in the late 1920s and '30s, worked so well that it became a standard business tool for nearly every major corporation. It has been used by the everyday household names below, all of whom have been my clients:

- Avis

- Samsung

- DHL

- Mazda

- KLM

- TWA

- Levitz Furniture

- Over 5,000 radio and TV stations in the United States

- Carnival Cruise Lines

- Air France

- Sheraton

- Lufthansa

The list goes on. But the point is they all trade! And this is another one of the secrets that only a limited amount of "inner-circle" people know. But as the business of barter grows and more and more people learn about trade clubs, you will have access to more and more people.

In fact, when you watch TV every night, you will never know which ads were paid with trade versus cash. They look the same and are transparent, but up to one-third of the media placements can be on trade at any point in time. And you will never know!

The Fine Art of Triangulation

We agree that can be difficult to go it alone, especially when you are new to the world of barter trade. You do not have a track record and are not yet trusted. And this is why it would be best to "cut your teeth" in a trade club.

Again, this does not mean that we recommend that you do not consider direct trade. You certainly should, and many of you reading this book can certainly do this, if you have something that you think someone wants and can get to the right person.

But even then you may find a situation where what you have is not something that someone else wants or needs.

Going back to our earlier example, if you went to your local Walmart store and offered the checkout associate ten hours of your time as a plumber for $1,000 worth of shopping, you may be escorted out of the store for two reasons:

1. You are not talking to the right person.

2. You have not been able to "triangulate."

What you need to do is get to the person at your local Walmart who writes the checks and then find out what they need done in the next thirty days.

Let's say that they need janitorial services, because customers are complaining about the toilets. You now call all the janitorial services in your area and cut a deal with them to do $1,000 worth of plumbing for them in lieu of them taking care of Walmart's janitorial services, valued at $1,000.

There is nothing wrong with this. Perfectly legal, and everyone wins. This process is called triangulation.

INSIDE SECRET #35

Triangulation is when you bring a third party in to complete the barter transaction, resolving the issue of not having what the other party wants.

It is a very simple and creative way to solve the problem of "I don't have what someone else needs." These types of triangulation deals are easy to do and are done all the time; you are only limited by your imagination in the types of triangulations you can do.

But I Have Nothing to Trade!

Barter trade, as you are starting to see, is an immensely powerful business tool that can give you leverage very quickly.

INSIDE SECRET #36

Once you understand how to use scrip, dating, float, breakage, and triangulation together, you will become unstoppable—and among the top financiers in the world! Because now you can put together whatever type of deal you want!

But the linear thinkers reading this book may still be a little skeptical. They may say, "All well and good, but I have nothing to trade!"

Our answer would be, if you can't sell it for cash, you may not even be able to sell it for trade. To trade, you need something to trade. To sell something, you need something to sell, something that is of value to others—irrespective of whether it is a cash or trade deal.

And this is one of the reasons we love trade so much. Trade, if you are business person, forces you to develop products and services that are valuable to others. If you are an individual, it may make you go back to college to get some skill sets that you can trade with or sell and are valuable to others.

INSIDE SECRET #37

Trade does not replace cash; it is just another way to pay. It is simply another tool or avenue for you that allows you to do more. It is a very creative way to take advantage of your excess, time, inventory, or equipment.

But having said that, we know that we know:

INSIDE SECRET #38

Everyone has something to trade. If you look hard enough, you will find it!

This could be your

- Time
- Talents
- Inventory
- Products
- Services
- Specialist knowledge
- And more

We all have something that is of value to someone else. And another reason that we love barter trade is that it will make you think really hard about yourself and your business, and what you have that may be desirable to others. It makes you take an audit or do a very detailed self-assessment.

If you are an independent professional, you probably have at least a few spare hours in your week that you could trade for something you need or want. If you are a lawyer, you may need some carpet for your office, so you may join a trade club and do some legal work for a few hours (i.e., help someone in the club set up a corporation), and in return gain credits to hire a carpenter who is a member of the trade club to lay the carpet you need in your office.

You may be a hotel with excess or unused inventory (i.e., rooms) that you can trade with a local radio station for airtime; you have already seen examples of this.

You can also make money by trading goods and services that you don't even own! All you need to do is borrow, access, or take control of other people's products, services, or inventory (OPP, OPS, OPI, etc.).

You can get a fee for putting a deal together, such as:

- A percentage from each party
- A percentage of the savings from each party
- A percentage of the profits
- Or whatever you can negotiate

Since barter trade is so misunderstood, you can help other people trade and make a good living yourself. This is how I made my fortune. In most cases, barter agents, like Hollywood agents, make more than the people they represent!

You could go to a local car dealer in your area and ask them which cars they are having a real problem selling. They would give you the five cars that have not been selling in trade for the equivalent amount of advertising credits that you would give them. Since the assets are idle, the car dealer would probably be motivated to do a deal with you—and happy to see them go, especially if he is getting full retail.

Now you go to a radio station and tell them that you want to buy $50,000 worth of advertising, but pay with four cars valued at $40,000. You keep one car as your commission. The media always pays the commission in a barter trade, and normal commissions are 15 to 20 percent. So you put the deal together and walk away with a car worth $10,000, without owning anything, controlling anything, or having anything to barter!

Radio stations can always use cars as part of a competition, or they can "cash-convert" them (i.e., sell them for cash) to friends of the station. And they would run the airtime exactly as if they paid cash, based on what is available. Although you pay in trade, you get the same rights and privileges as cash!

So to say that you don't have anything to barter or trade is a myth. You just need to start to think creatively and out-of-the-box. Which is what this book is all about, right?

MYTH 4: NOBODY BARTERS THESE DAYS. BARTER IS BASICALLY HAGGLING.

When you think of barter, you may be thinking of the Stone Age, when a doctor traded his or her services for chickens. But as you have seen with the concept of scrip, barter has evolved into a highly sophisticated financial instrument. And we assure you that with trade clubs, barter trade is alive and well in our modern-day society!

According to the International Reciprocal Trade Association (IRTA), almost half a million small businesses today use commercial barter exchanges each year. Currently, commercial barter is a more than $16-billion-a-year industry in the United States and can include anything and everything from "you mow my lawn, and I'll do your taxes" to Pepsi accepting shipments of vodka in exchange for distribution rights because they did not want to be paid in rubles.

> We have found in our experience that it is not uncommon for businesses who regularly barter to receive 10 percent of their income from barter sales.

It is not uncommon for up to 25 percent of magazine advertising to be based on trade, not cash! Barter is very well understood by the media as a creative and profitable way of doing business (as its origins, as you have seen, came from the media).

Barter is not haggling. Many people confuse the two terms. Let us make a clear distinction here. Haggling is negotiating for a lower price; barter, on the other hand, is about exchanging value for value, or goods and services that have equal value to both parties. Remember the barter equation, $x = y$, for the trade to be fair.

To think that we don't barter anymore is simply not true! So many people are doing it! And this is the secret that we are letting you in on! According to the World Trade Exchange, barter is a $50 billion global industry. And they point out that over 400,000 US companies barter each year. This includes most of the Fortune 500 companies. Globally, governments, large corporations, and individuals engage in over $1 trillion of barter business per year. Every major government has a department of trade and industry. B2B (business to business) cashless transactions across North America is big business. Barter exchanges are flourishing. Trade transactions at Bizx.com, a major barter exchange, have gone from $30.6 million in 2006 to $63.8 million in 2009. Large trade clubs can processes $100 million a year in gross merchandise and have up to 24,000 members. You can trade with virtually every type of business if you are a member of the club. And this is just one of the several hundred barter trade clubs in North America. Amazon now even barters with you; you can trade your goods and services for Amazon gift cards.

Sorry, We Don't Trade

One of the best ways to show you how a few simple words can shift the dynamics of barter trade is to share with you my (Dave's) story of Mazda.

In the early 1970s, I had the opportunity to work with Mazda. They had several hundred Mazda Cosmos. They could not sell these cars; they had been sitting, losing value.

I was in the Los Angeles office with the executives of Mazda, and I explained to them all the potential benefits of trade that you have read about so far. I offered them advertising as a trade for the Cosmos. I was prepared to take them off their hands and offer the equivalent in advertising time that would help them sell other vehicles. And I was prepared to pay full rate, not a discounted rate, for these cars. Their response?

"We do not trade, because we may lose face."

The Mazda executives were very fearful that if they traded, they would lose face in the industry, and the competition would say, "Mazda could not sell cars, so they had to trade them." Like trade was a bad thing, just like giving away cars or selling at a discount.

I left the office and was on the freeway—then it hit me. They thought that trade was a bad, five-letter word! So I turned the car around, went back to the office, and when I got back into the meeting room, I told them that I changed my mind. I just wanted to "buy" the Cosmos but I would pay for it in the form of advertising. Their response? They said great, and we had a deal!

 # INSIDE SECRET #39

Always tell people that you would like to buy, not trade. Replacing the five-letter word "trade" with a three-letter word "buy" will always secure your deal!

Yes, there is still a social stigma around the words "barter" or "trade." But you can quickly get around this by changing it to the word "buy," and you pay in trade.

Mazda was able to get rid of inventory that it could not normally sell using conventional methods. It traded it for advertising that it was able to use to sell its other product lines that were selling. Which was a very smart thing to do. And as we have said before, both parties win, and there is no catch.

What happened to the Cosmos? I was able to give them to radio stations around the country for equivalent airtime. The radio stations loved having the Cosmos. One person's excess inventory can be another person's treasure in barter trade.

MYTH 5: BARTER IS ILLEGAL, OR A TAX-EVASION STRATEGY.

Barter is not illegal, nor is it a tax-evasion strategy. It is simply a very smart business strategy that gives you immense leverage. Barter predates money and was the way we used to do business with each other before so-called cash emerged. Although Uncle Sam was probably around in those days also! The primary reasons we moved to cash are that it is convenient, universal, and fast. Cash allows for instantaneous transactions.

Barter transactions typically take longer, as you need to negotiate to ensure both parties gain fair and equal value from the transaction. But at the same time, they are immensely profitable for both parties involved, if done correctly, and everyone wins. And there is no catch!

 # INSIDE SECRET #40

Barter is a business tool, just like any other.

Tools can be used correctly or misused. There are people who will abuse the power of the barter system. We know many cases where employees have "by accident" figured out how the barter system works and how profitable it can be.

A friend of ours runs a franchise fast-food outlet, and when one of his employees left, he had to run the franchise himself for while. When he came back to run his franchise again, he found that some customers would come in and, when asked to pay, simply say, "No, this is on trade."

What had happened was that his old employee had been trading with local business owners for goods and services, haircuts, meals, car repairs, etc. And nothing was being put on the books of either party.

Yes, this is illegal and wrong. A trade is a sale just like any other sale, and taxes are due. And, of course, the employees should be selling for cash, not trade.

These types of examples are not uncommon, and this is why you may think that barter is illegal, bad, or wrong. Again, barter trade is a business tool, and just like any other tool, it can be misused.

With respect to taxes, barter is recognized by the IRS as a legal way of doing business. We will be talking extensively about how to handle your barter transactions from a tax perspective in great detail in a later chapter.

The most important thing to remember is:

> All barter "income" must be declared just like cash revenues. It only becomes illegal if you do not declare your trades. And if you do not make any income on a barter trade (i.e., it is used for a business expense), then there is no tax due.

A simple way to remember how to handle a trade transaction is to remember that what you receive counts as income, and what you supply counts as an expense.

Just remember that barter trade is the same as a cash transaction (you just don't pay in cash) and must be documented like a cash transaction. If you do that, you will not have any problem with Uncle Sam.

MYTH 6: BARTER PRODUCTS AND SERVICES ARE SUB-STANDARD.

There is a misconception that if you trade, you get a sub-standard product. And people who do barter trade are not trustworthy. This is also not true.

 **INSIDE SECRET #41**

With barter, you have the same rights and privileges as cash; you just don't pay with cash!

It is estimated that nearly 75 percent of the Fortune 500 do barter trade, and you have seen the list of companies that have been my clients. They are all household names.

In a barter trade, you are offered the same products or services that are offered to cash-paying customers. Doing barter trade does not mean you are dealing with shady (i.e., untrustworthy) people. If something is not a good cash trade, it probably is also not a good barter trade. The only difference is the form of payment, which is your goods or services! This is a very simple but powerful distinction in mindset that you need to make if you are to be successful in barter.

You just need to treat a barter-trade transaction the same as a cash transaction, and you will not fall into the trap of thinking a barter transaction is sub-standard. You are exchanging value for value. Again, $x = y$. Barter is all about equivalent value exchange.

For barter trade to work successfully, both parties need to honor the credit.

When you trade with a media station for airtime, the station will show you exactly when your time will run; you are not given any leftover space. You should and will be treated as a cash-paying customer. The only difference is that you are not paying them in cash, but in exchange for the goods and services that you may offer.

As I pointed out previously, when you see a TV ad, you cannot tell if it was paid for from trade or with cash. You would be surprised to know that some of the ads you love are paid for in trade dollars. A major corporation may pay thousands of dollars for a sixty-second commercial, while a local pizza company may simply pay with pizza. But it is something that you will never know. The only person that knows how the ad was paid for is the owner or principal of the media station.

Barter goods and services are not sub-standard; they are of equivalent standard to cash. In the Mazda deal, they got full retail for the cars—they were not discounted! You should never discount your product or service as well. Barter is always done at full retail!

MYTH 7: BARTER MEANS YOU ARE GETTING THINGS FOR FREE.

One of the most important things to remember about barter is that you are not getting things for free. "No cash" does not mean "free!" It just means that you are not using cash as a form of payment, but your goods and services.

We hope by now that you have mastered the barter equation $x = y$. You are exchanging value for value. You are exchanging what you have, which may be product, service, or ideas, for what you want.

In the early 1970s, Robert Allen came up with the concept of "no-money-down real estate." This became very popular, but the key to his concept was barter—being able to trade for the down payment! It did not mean you did not pay any down payment; you just came up with creative ways of providing it besides paying cash! His book became one of the bestselling finance books of all time, and what Bob was teaching was barter trade!

In summary, consider bartering for anything that you normally would pay cash for! Make a list of items that you personally buy, for yourself and your company, and then look to purchase the same things "cash free" or " cashless." This means finding people whom you can trade with directly, or joining a local trade club.

Start small, and as you build your confidence, you can do larger transactions.

THINGS TO REMEMBER FROM THIS CHAPTER

- Treat a barter trade like cash.

- Anything that is not being used can be put to good use with a trading mentality.

- Barter clubs are a simple and easy way to get to know how barter works.

- Triangulate if the person you want to barter with does not want what you have.

- Change "trade" to "buy," and you will trade a lot more!

- Barter trade is recognized by the IRS as a legal way of doing business.

- The barter equation is $x = y$. It is all about value exchange.

chapter four

— 4 —

Have No Fear, Even if the IRS Is Here

The hardest thing in the world to understand is the income tax.

Albert Einstein

I (Dave) am no expert in barter taxation, and I am not qualified to provide any professional taxation advice. What is provided in this chapter is a general guideline that I use, and I have been doing barter trade for forty years at WAGI Advertising. In fact, I have assisted the IRS in audits of fair-market-value appraisals. You should consult your tax advisor for any questions concerning barter or taxes as they relate to your specific transactions.

Yes, the biggest question that always comes up with respect to barter trade is how to handle Uncle Sam and taxes. There appears to be a general misunderstanding of barter and tax implications. Most people think that barter is some form of loophole to get out of paying taxes, or it is illegal. Maybe some kind of "underground economy." You will find that most of the people who have issues with barter trade did not report all the earnings or keep adequate records of the transactions that they have made.

Your barter transactions will usually take place in a few ways:

- As a hobby

- As a business, one on one

- Through a third party—i.e., a modern-day barter exchange

We will discuss each shortly. But the most important thing to remember is that bartering is legal and recognized by the IRS as a legitimate way of doing business.

"Just because I can leap tall buildings
in a single bound doesn't mean
I can understand the tax code."

The best business advice I can give you with respect to barter trade is to remember:

 # INSIDE SECRET #42

The real secret to barter and to the way to handle all your barter transactions is to treat barter like cash, which it really is. If you have good recordkeeping habits, you will never have a problem with the IRS.

> Barter trade *is not* a tax-evasion strategy. It is a leverage strategy to get more out of your current marketing expenditure.

There are no tax advantages or real disadvantages to bartering. It is just the same as cash; you just don't pay with cash. Bartering dollars are considered the same as cash dollars, as far as Uncle Sam is concerned. So trading should be considered a marketing tool, not a tax tool.

BARTER AS A HOBBY

You may want to start with barter as a hobby—i.e., you have a few items in your garage that you would like to exchange with a friend for some products or services that you may need (for example, you might want to exchange your fridge for someone else's TV). But the IRS counts this type of trade as "personal use," and officially, you have generated reportable income. So any personal trade needs to be reported by both parties to the IRS as income. Based on the "fair market value" of the goods or services exchanged and the tax basis, each party will pay the respective amount of taxes. This would be reported in the annual tax filing as part of the income received for the year. You will see an example shortly of how the IRS would like you to handle this.

Remember that barter or trade dollars are identical to real dollars for tax reporting. If you conduct any direct barter—barter for another's products or services—you will have to report the fair market value of the products or services you received on your tax return. Although no money is exchanged, the trading of services or goods represents income in the eyes of the IRS and therefore must be reported as income and taxed as income.

BARTER FOR BUSINESS

If you are really serious about barter, then it needs to become a business for you, and you need to run it like a professional business with adequate bookkeeping and records. I would recommend that you start by joining a trade club.

Join a Local or National Barter Exchange

We will be talking about barter clubs and trade clubs extensively in chapter 7. They basically act as your broker and take care of all the paperwork. Here you "bank credit" for your product or services, and you can then draw against these credits. Should you join a professional trade club, they will issue you a 1099-B ("Proceeds from Broker and Barter Exchange Transactions") at the end of the fiscal year, and this is what you need to file as part of your tax return.

The amount shown in 1099-B Box 3, Bartering, is the amount of your barter transactions proceeds. This is generally reportable as income and must be included on your tax return. Barter exchanges have an annual obligation to report your bartering proceeds to the IRS.

The #1 Secret to Barter and Taxation: Keep Good Records!

Many business owners fear that if they engage in barter, they are on the radar for audit from the IRS. But the IRS has very well-established rules and understands that barter is a normal part of any business practice. In my opinion, you are not any more likely to get audited if you barter than if you are doing business with cash and credit.

The only time you are likely to get in trouble with the IRS is the same as with a cash business: because you do not have full documentation. Again, I hate to sound like a broken record, but treat trade like cash. Assess a fair-market value to the goods and services you either buy or sell. Barter, like cash, has associated tax reporting, accounting, and recordkeeping responsibilities.

McHUMOR.com by T. McCracken

"I haven't found anything wrong with your books yet, but it's OK for you to go ahead and worry a bit longer."

In barter-trade transactions, you will be receiving or delivering a product or services. The simplest way to receive products and services is to keep all the trade invoices for any items that you might receive that show the fair-market value. For products you create and deliver, keep all the sales receipts—again, at fair-market value.

Barter is a sale just like any other sale you may make; the only difference is that you do not pay in cash. If you sell something for cash, you usually generate an invoice; in the same way, when you sell something for barter you should keep records of your barter invoices. If you buy something, you would get a sales receipt. In the case of barter, you simply mark the receipt as a barter-trade receipt. This will keep the recordkeeping simple and straightforward. Whether you maintain your books and records manually or

McHUMOR.com by T. McCracken

"There's really no need for confusion.
Part 95 of section 33 of article Q
in the formula quite clearly states ... "

use one of the many accounting and tax software packages on the market today, you need to keep and record all the information about your barter transactions.

Clearly mark or file all barter income and expense documents as "bartering," and retain all original source documents pertaining to your barter transactions:

- Sales receipts and invoices

- Barter exchange statements and Forms 1099-B

WHAT THE IRS SAYS ABOUT BARTER

The following quote is taken directly from the IRS website:

> "Bartering is the trading of one product or service for another. Usually there is no exchange of cash. It is the most ancient form of commerce. Any business owner or professional who has a product or service to offer can barter."
> *Source: IRS Bartering Tax Center*

The IRS understands barter very well and has defined rules for handling barter trade. Early in the 1970s, the IRS actually formalized its rules on taxing bartered income. Now the IRS taxes barter transactions in dollars and cents, even though no money changes hands. This means you have to keep full records on the trades you make, so they can be properly taxed. The IRS measures bartered exchanges by using the market price of the goods or services someone receives. In a swap, both parties have to list the market value of what they received as taxable income.

INSIDE SECRET #43

The most important thing to remember about barter and taxes is that barter is exactly like any other business transaction; the only difference is that you do not pay with cash. The recordkeeping and documentation is the same as if you did.

For more information on barter and taxation, visit the IRS Tax Center.

THINGS TO REMEMBER FROM THIS CHAPTER

- Barter is perfectly legal and is not a tax-evasion strategy.
- Treat barter income as cash income.
- Keep good records!
- Consult the IRS Barter Tax Center.

PART 2:
Mechanics of Barter Trade

chapter five

— 5 —

Trade Terms and Terminology

*If you talk to a man in a language he understands,
that goes to his head. If you talk to him in his
language, that goes to his heart.*

Nelson Mandela

A s you are starting to see, barter is more than simply exchanging goods and services. The way that you exchange them leads to the creation of a financial instrument, and this has tax implications—after all, you are doing a business transaction.

In the next chapter, I (Dave) am going to show you real examples of barter-trade deals that my company WAGI has done over a forty-year history, but before we get there, I want to ground you in the terms and terminology of barter, so you have a solid foundation and don't get lost in all the jargon when we really get into the meat of things in the next chapter.

You already have a basic understanding of the four pillars of barter trade: scrip, dating, float, and breakage.

When you issue a *scrip*, it has with it an accompanying timeline, which is called the *dating*. The dollar amount of the scrip is the float that is available. And the unused portion of a scrip is called the *breakage*.

Now we will continue to build on these barter building blocks by introducing some new terms, while at the same time reviewing

McHUMOR.com by T. McCracken

"I was in a computer terminology class a whole week before I realized it wasn't German 101."

and revisiting the old ones, to ensure that you are well grounded in the tools that barter professionals use.

After reviewing this chapter, you will really start to sound like a true barter pro and amaze people in the world of finance! And become one of the top financiers in the world.

SOFT DOLLARS

This is a term that you will hear very frequently in the world of barter trade. Very early on in my career, one of my first accounts was a hotel near Los Angeles International Airport (LAX) that was owned by an Englishman. I proposed the idea of trading rooms at his hotel for radio airtime. The man was very smart; as soon as he heard the proposition, he said, "Oh, so you want to trade 'soft dollars' (i.e., empty rooms for advertising). Soft dollars are very attractive to me."

And of course, the deal went ahead. A soft dollar is a term to describe the barter scrip. As the barter scrip is not legal tender that is backed by the US Government, it is legal tender backed by you!

In the world of barter, your unit of currency is the scrip or soft dollar. Some barter exchanges call these "barter bucks."

Another way to define soft dollars is simply using your goods and services as a form of payment.

HARD DOLLARS

Hard dollars are essentially "hard cash, checks, or credit cards." It is what you and I know as conventional cash that is backed by the treasury department and theoretically tied to gold.

SCRIP

This is one of the secrets only known to five hundred barter professionals around the world. This is what takes a very simple transaction between two people and converts it into a powerful leverage tool.

You probably now understand scrip. A scrip is a simple agreement between two people who provide goods or services to each other. Theoretically, it is a legal agreement. But most scrips rarely mention what happens if either party defaults on their obligation. So barter by nature is really based on trust between the two parties.

The scrip is basically an IOU. It is only legal tender at your place of business, as you are standing behind the currency that you created. Scrips are basically "futures," as they will be used at some time in the future. They allow you to get what you want right now and pay at some time in the future!

In the old days, people would do business on a handshake. The scrip simply makes the handshake more formal.

 **INSIDE SECRET #44**

A scrip is a very simple document that outlines what you will give and what you will get in return. Both parties sign, and trust that both parties will honor their portion of the credits. Some people call scrip funny money!

Now this may surprise you, that anyone would do barter transactions based on such a simple document. But as we pointed out earlier, barter trade is based on honesty and integrity.

Such scrips have been used to do millions of dollars' worth of businesses. You really don't need anyone's approval to write a scrip or come to an trade agreement with them.

On the next page is an example of a very simple barter scrip that I (Ali) use.

The scrip can be as simple or as complicated as you like. Most barter-trade deals are done with very simple scrips, like the one shown above. Many are actually done on a handshake. For my (Dave's) business, when I am trading advertising on one of my radio stations with a local merchant, I would issue a scrip as shown on the following page.

CASHLESS TRANSACTIONS/"NO-CASH" ADVERTISING

The end result of a barter trade is a cashless transaction, as the goods and services become the unit of currency and no cash changes hands.

I, _____, on this day, _____ do hereby
agree to perform

The following Service:

Type of Service
_____

Amount of Service
_____

Time Period in which Service is to be Performed:
_____
_____

Other Agreements
_____

In exchange for:
_____

Party Receiving   Party Receiving
Service: Service:

_____   _____
Name   Name

_____   _____
Address   Address

_____   _____
Phone   Phone

_____   _____
Signature   Signature

This Document (is) (is not) transferable.

Many think that it is free, but what we are doing is simply promoting barter trade. It allows business owners to increase their sales without spending any cash! A very desirable proposition.

You can purchase advertising for "no cash," or by using a cashless transaction. We offer cashless advertising at WAGI. The flyer on the next page is our promotion piece.

NO CASH ADVERTISING
WHAT IS NO CASH ADVERTISING?

NO CASH ADVERTISING MAKES IT POSSIBLE FOR YOU TO PROMOTE
YOUR BUSINESS ON RADIO, TV, OUTDOOR, AND PRINT WITHOUT USING
CASH. THE ADVERTISING IS PAID WITH GOODS AND/OR SERVICES
INSTEAD OF CASH.

HOW DOES USING NO CASH ADVERTISING BENEFIT ME?
SINCE YOU ARE USING YOUR GOODS AND/OR SERVICES TO PAY FOR
PART OR ALL THE COSTS, THE ACTUAL CASH COST IS MUCH LESS. ALSO
YOU ARE INCREASING YOUR SALES WITHOUT USING CASH.

WAGI IS A COMPANY OWNED BY DAVE AND LOLA WAGENVOORD AND
HAS ARRANGED MORE THAN $500 MILLION OF CASH ADVERTISING
THROUGHOUT THE WORLD.

WHAT IF I DON'T HAVE ANYTHING TO PAY WITH OTHER THAN CASH?

USE WAGI DISCOUNT ADVERTISING.

DISCOUNT ADVERTISING IS MADE AVAILABLE TO YOU BY USING PRE-
OWNED CREDITS THROUGH WAGI CONTACTS. THE DISCOUNTS ARE 25%
TO 60% LESS THAN YOU WOULD PAY AS A REGULAR CUSTOMER. BOTH
NO CASH AND DISCOUNT ADVERTISING CAN BE USED WITH RADIO,
LOCAL AND NATIONAL (TV, CABLE, SPOT, AND NETWORK) PRINT,
MAGAZINE, NEWSPAPERS, AND DIRECT MAIL. OUTDOOR, LOCAL AND
NATIONAL.

TO FIND OUT MORE, CALL DAVE AT 727-424-4991 FOR A PROPOSAL TO
LOWER YOUR COST OF ADVERTISING.

HARD COSTS

Hard costs can only be covered with hard dollars—i.e., you need cash. Maybe the plumber cannot trade his gas costs, for example, as he needs money to pay for these because no one will trade with him for these. This is an important point. In most cases, people may not trade their hard costs with you, because who they do business with (i.e., their vendors) may require cash only.

If I am a plumber, and my profit margin is $100 on $200 worth of work, I can always "trade out" the $100 profit I have, as that is cash that I can keep. In business, your soft costs are usually the profit you make, and that can always be traded out.

 # INSIDE SECRET #45

You can always trade the soft costs out of a deal, once the hard costs are covered.

SIMULTANEOUS CLOSE/CLOSE-END TRADE (WHEN X IS NOT EQUAL TO Y)

The people who fear barter do so because they think that x will not equal y—i.e., I give you something, but you do not give me the equivalent value back in return! Not because you are a bad person, but maybe your business goes through a tough time, and you go bankrupt and cannot repay your obligation.

Yes, this has happened to me also. I have done deals with people where I gave them (or found them) the much-needed advertising that they needed to make their businesses successful, only to later find out that they went bankrupt! So x did not equal y.

And I was never paid my credits, because in bankruptcy court, the trade credits are one of the first things to be taken off the books.

Does this make barter bad? No! We keep saying the same thing, that a barter deal is no different than a cash deal; you just don't pay with cash. Any cash-paying client could also go out of business. There is an old saying in the barter world: if the person is no good for cash, he is no good for trade!

INSIDE SECRET #46

As in a cash deal, do your due diligence with the people with whom you are going to barter to ensure that x = y, or that what you give is equal in value to what you get.

Now you understand why, if you called a media station directly and asked to trade for advertising, they would not deal with you directly. Just like in life and business, we only like to deal with people whom we know, like, and trust!

Sure, any media station in the country would deal with me; WAGI has been in the business for forty years, and I am well respected for being honest and ethical. A lot of people have made a lot of money from my deals. Just like in any business, it takes time to build your brand. Ali defines "brand" very well in his book, *Get Your Black Belt in Marketing* (www.blackbeltinmarketing.com). A "brand" is "trust." People need to trust you to do business with you.

However, there is a way to overcome the issue of x not being equal to y. You simply do a simultaneous close—i.e., you get what you want at the same time as the party you are dealing with gets what they want.

Scan this with your smartphone QR app.

For example, if WAGI is offered furniture for advertising on my media stations, I ask them to deliver all the furniture to a warehouse, and the same day I run all their advertising. This is what we call a simultaneous close. Just like when you buy a house and it goes through escrow.

This may not work in all situations, such as if you are unable to consume all the

goods you want at once (i.e., $10,000 worth of food). But it is an alternative.

Again, the basis of barter and of business is that you are dealing with people who are honest and trustworthy.

 **INSIDE SECRET #47**

If someone is no good for a cash deal, it is also likely that they are no good for a barter-trade deal. Treat trade the same as cash!

TRIANGULATION

We have covered this earlier, and you may see triangulation operate as part of the deals that we will be showing you shortly. The diagram below shows how it works.

You can always find a third person to solve your problem and the equation. Just look in any vendor directory or the yellow pages, and start offering your product or service to them, so they can provide you with the product or service you need to trade with someone else.

 **INSIDE SECRET #48**

You use triangulation to get what you want when you don't have what the other person needs.

In a triangulation deal, you have three parties: the buyer, the seller, and the customer.

BREAKAGE

Breakage was covered earlier. When stores issue you a gift card, this is basically a scrip, and any unused portion of a scrip ends up as profit for the person that issued the card. How often have you received a gift card for fifty dollars and only used forty-eight or forty-nine? Then you probably threw the card away. You basically threw two dollars back to the vendor's bank account as breakage.

Breakage is big business in business! Those two dollars quickly add up to several million dollars, just like pennies quickly make dollars. Ali tells me that he never carries any change, only notes. He gives this change to his son, who has at least thirty dollars from pocket money a month from all those pennies, quarters, dimes, and nickels! Now he is saving up to buy his next iPhone from Ali's breakage!

Smart businesses know their numbers and factor breakage into their financial plan.

You will soon see numerous examples of how breakage played an important part in a lot of the deals that I've done. I just knew my numbers and factored them into the barter calculation.

DATING

No, not romantic dating! But barter dating, which is simply the terms and conditions you apply to the scrip. When you issue a scrip, you will usually put the period that the goods and services can be used or provided—i.e., its expiration length. If someone trusts you, they will allow you to make the dating long, as they know they can call on you to honor the scrip at any time.

But this gives barter a unique position versus cash.

 **INSIDE SECRET #49**

In barter, the longer you take to pay, the less you pay—unlike with cash, where the longer you take to pay, the more you end up paying! A dollar today is worth more than a dollar tomorrow, because it can be reinvested!

FLOAT

The float is the result of not paying all at once for your product or service. It is the amount of money that you have available, or "free cash." Several years ago, American Express issued traveler's cheques, most of which had a dating of nearly a year. Most people would buy the traveler's cheques in advance and just not use all of the scrip or voucher that was issued.

This allowed American Express the use of the funds, or float, which could be placed into short-term securities. Which made them a lot of money!

INSIDE SECRET #50

Barter not only allows you to conserve cash (by not using it) but also to make cash by cash conversions.

The people who best understand floats are banks and financial institutions, who make a large sum of money on short-term securities (i.e., investing money overnight). Basically they make their living "on the float." Or the float keeps them afloat. No pun intended, of course!

CASH CONVERSION

Through your bartering endeavors, you will acquire many products, goods, and services. Now, you may not have an immediate need for these. So what do you do with all this inventory? You cash-convert it. Yes, it means exactly what it says—convert what you have to cash. The best way to think of cash conversion is that it's like taking your jewelry to a pawn shop. They examine it and pay you cash. You just need to find someone who will buy what you want for cash.

INSIDE SECRET #51

Some barter experts refer to cash conversion as "trade liquidation."

Several years ago, Chrysler traded a Spanish television network 192 cars for advertising. The network then turned around and sold the cars to their employees at a 30 percent discount over what the cars normally "stickered" for to their employees. The employees loved this, as they could not get this discount anywhere else! The average value of each car was $10,000. The television network received $1,920,000 (192 x $10,000) in real cash from the cash conversion. And what did it cost them? Unsold airtime, which cost them nothing (time that probably would have gone unused and thus would have produced zero revenue, but they were smart enough to trade it).

 INSIDE SECRET #52

The tool that generates cash in barter trade is cash conversion. Taking the inventory that you acquire through your trading activities and selling it for cash!

Oh, just to complete the story. Forty-five of the cars that the station acquired were traded to a television transmitter manufacturer in exchange for a half-million dollars' worth of transmitter equipment that permitted the station to open up a new full-power UHF station in San Francisco—without using any cash. Ahead of the competition, the station was sold for $400 million. All this could not have been done if they hadn't understood the mechanics of how to put together a barter deal. And of course, the deal made the owners very wealthy in the process!

RECYCLED DOLLARS

You will often hear the term "recycled dollars" in the trading community, and the reason is that all goods and services are reused in a barter trade.

"Green economics" is the new buzzword!

Barter is all about conserving resources, building community, and keeping no-longer-needed belongings from going to waste.

 **INSIDE SECRET #53**

Barter is about going green! It is green economics—recycling and reusing what you have. Nothing goes to waste! Go Green! Go Barter!

If you look at our current system of doing commerce or business, which is "take my money and give me this," it creates a real disconnect between the giver and receiver. There is no appreciation of one's work, time, or individual qualities, because what we are receiving is no longer human but merely product or service. The "help" element is removed. But products and services were developed so we might help each other.

On the other hand, when you barter and trade, the transaction is slowed, so there is time to appreciate another's talent and help, and there is beauty in sharing your own talent.

We believe that fulfillment in life comes less from "look what I got from you" and more from "thank you for helping me solve my problem"—or moving away from making transactions for profit to making transactions to help each other solve mutual problems.

There is a kind of dignity and nobility associated with a true barter transaction.

A recent study by Goodwill Industries found that 23.8 billion pounds of clothing and textiles end up in US landfills every year! And that is just in the United States alone.

According to the USDA, 27 percent of all the food produced each year is lost at the retail, consumer, and food-service levels. We throw away about 263,013,699 pounds of food a day—every single day! And much of what is wasted actually is just surplus food. It is perfectly edible.

The founding principle of barter trade is to use everything you have—products, services, time, talents—for trade! It is all about recycling and reusing everything!

One of the favorite terms of barter experts is "recycled dollars." This is when what you spend ends up coming back to you.

How can this be possible? Well, when you issue a scrip, it is only valid at your place of business, so it in essence forces people to do business with you. The dollars that you spend for goods and services will always come back to you and your pocket.

Why do you think that most stores would prefer to give you store credit rather than cash? For the same reason: to be able to recycle the dollars back into their business.

Several years ago, the City of Palm Springs made a trade deal with the media across the United States. But for the media to redeem the credit, the City of Palm Springs required the media to travel to Palm Springs—i.e., it could only be redeemed at merchants in Palm Springs. Yes, they figured out how to "recycle" dollars!

A lot of the real-world examples that I (Dave) have done do involve the recycling of dollars. Now you know what this means.

RATIOS

One of the big things you will hear barter experts talk about is ratios. What they are referring to is what they got for what they gave.

 **INSIDE SECRET #54**

In barter trade, the ratio is what you got for what you traded!

Yes, up to now, we have said that x = y for barter; you should get back what you were given for the trade to be fair. And this is true in 99 percent of all cases. But as you master barter trade, you will be able to negotiate for better than 1:1 ratios!

If what you have is very desirable to the person you are trading, then you can often get a better than 1:1 ratio. Travel and cars are perfect examples. You can always trade better than 1:1 when it is a deal that involves a car. So if you are a car dealer, that means you can get twice as much advertising than you are paying for! This is called a 2:1 ratio, which means you just doubled your purchasing power.

Ratios are always negotiable and depend on the desirability of the product. You don't have to settle for 1:1. This is just the starting point. You will see the incredible power of ratios in the next chapter.

THINGS TO REMEMBER FROM THIS CHAPTER

- There are many tools that you can use to put together whatever type of barter trade deal you want. It now really boils down to your imagination and creativity on how to structure your deal.

- The scrip is the key tool for barter professionals.

- A barter deal is no different than a cash deal. Only deal with ethical people.

- Barter not only conserves cash but also generates it, using cash conversions.

- x = y is a "fair trade" and a 1:1 ratio.

- The more desirable your offering, the higher the ratio.

chapter six

— 6 —

It's Real!
Real-World Case Studies

*If you want to be a master at anything, study what
masters before you have done. Learn to do exactly
what they have done. Have the courage to do it.
And you too can soon be a master just like them!*

Anonymous

By now you should have a good understanding of what barter trade is and its terms and terminology. You are now ready to see the true power of barter in action, and we will do this by sharing real-world case studies.

SUGARED WATER FOR VODKA. FAIR TRADE?

You would actually be surprised by all the companies that use barter as an important part of their overall business portfolio and growth strategy. The best place to start is the most classic barter deal of the twentieth century, which Pepsi did with the former USSR in 1972.

In 1972, Pepsi was the first foreign product sold in the former USSR. However, instead of selling their product for cash, Pepsi entered into a barter-trade agreement with the Soviet government and took payment in the form of Stolichnaya ("Stoli") Russian vodka. This worked perfectly, because at that time the Soviet

Union had limited access to foreign currency because they were not a major exporter.

In a conventional deal, Pepsi would have had to set up bottling plants and then sell their product for rubles, which they would then have to take to the central bank in exchange for dollars. However, at that time, the USSR did not have access to dollars, and so could not approve the sale of foreign products. The use of barter trade very cleverly got around the currency issue and enabled Pepsi to secure exclusive rights to the Stolichnaya name in the United States, not to mention establishing themselves in the massive Soviet market. A brilliant marketing move.

By 1990, the barter-trade deal reached a value of $3 billion, with Pepsi trading its product not only for vodka, but also for ocean-going freighters and tankers that were earmarked to be sold as scrap. By this point, Pepsi was not just selling syrup but was expanding in the fast-food business via its Pizza Hut franchise.

The barter agreement carried on through the end of the Cold War in the early 1990s. With the Soviet collapse, Coca-Cola was introduced to the Russian market and captured a significant market share, eventually overtaking Pepsi in 2005.

CAN I HAVE SOME FISH FOR SWEETENER?

In 1935, US pharmaceutical giant Monsanto sold saccharine to a company in China. When the company was unable to pay in cash, Monsanto took frozen mackerel in exchange and acquired an export market in the world's most populous country.

SOLVING THAILAND'S BEEF-SHORTAGE PROBLEM WITH BARTER

In 2002, the Thai government agreed to arrange a swap of 60,000 tonnes of excess rice for 300,000 South African cattle, avoiding a plunge in rice prices and solving its beef-shortage problem in one trade.

AIR MILES ARE ONE OF THE BEST FORMS OF TRADE!

One of the best real-world examples that shows how only those trained in barter trade can spot barter deals is the kind of loyalty program that nearly every major airline, hotel, and credit-card company offers.

If you give your loyalty to an airline by using them frequently, they will in return reward you with "air miles," or free travel. Now as we showed, the definition of barter or trade is simply a "cashless transaction." Neither you nor the airline exchanged any money, so air miles are one of the best forms of barter or trade that go unnoticed on the radar, except by people trained in barter!

All major hotels and many retailers also offer loyalty programs. Major hotels like Sheraton, Hilton, and Marriott offer reward programs that offer points for stays. These points can then be redeemed—or maybe a better word would be "traded"—for future stays.

They are trading your loyalty and recycling the dollars back into their business, which is what trade is ideal for. And it is also a very smart business move.

> Whenever a transaction occurs in business or in life, and no money changes hands, it is a trade!

HOW ABOUT A FREE MOVIE TICKET?

If you go to Fandango, a major online movie site, they will offer you a free movie ticket if you "test drive," or try, a promotion from one of their partners. This is again a trade: you trade your time to test drive an offer, and in return you get a movie ticket. No cash changes hands. Did you see this on the radar? Any movement of products or services without the movement of money is a trade transaction.

We hope by now you are starting to see how your time is actually the most valuable commodity you have. Most people make their money by trading their time for money; this is called a job. But your time, as you have seen, can be traded for virtually anything. Your time is very valuable! Manage it carefully. Trade it wisely!

HOW TO DO $500 MILLION WORTH OF TRADE

Over the past forty years, WAGI has done about half a billion dollars' worth of trade deals, with every type of company you can imagine, in every major industry.

Barter is real and continues to be used by nearly every major corporation in the United States and around the world. It is the modern way of doing business, and it's ideal in tough economic times.

Now I (Dave) am going to share with you some real-world case studies of deals I have put together that show how simple, creative, and extremely lucrative bartering can be. I hope that after studying these case studies your mind and imagination will start to open up to the possibilities that barter trade truly offers. For confidentiality reasons, I have had to remove the names of some of the companies, but you probably will recognize them. But I assure you that they are all real deals.

Our hope and desire is that you start to see what is possible. Yes, you can do these types of deals! Maybe not at the same level as I have, but with your own products and services at whatever level you feel comfortable with. Mindset is what it is all about. Start small; build confidence and credibility first. All you need to get started is the barter mindset, and the methods will follow naturally and automatically. Soon you will move from the "pay cash" mentality to the trade mentality, and stop reaching for your wallet and checkbook!

Our goal in writing this book is to spark your mind, imagination, and creativity so you can start to put together whatever type of deals you want. We really want you to start thinking differently about business and life. You cannot win the game of life doing what everyone else does; you need to think and act differently. If you do what everyone else does, you will get the same results. If you do different things, you may really surprise yourself!

A lot of the case studies we are going to present to you will make you step back, because they are approaches that are "not conventional." Both Ali and I pride ourselves on being creative, out-of-the-box thinkers.

When Henry Ford developed the first automobile, if he had asked people what they wanted, they would have said, "Faster horses." The only problem was that they did not exist! Instead he thought differently and came up with an automobile—which in the end was a faster horse! But he went about it in a different way.

We hope that after reading these case studies you will start to think and act differently and start to come up with your own creative deals. Once you master the basic concepts, you will soon start to see that all these deals involve the same fundamentals of barter trade: issuing scrips, ratios, and cash conversion, at some stage, to cash out. Some deals are a little more intricate than others. But all eventually boil down to good business practice, integrity, and basic common sense.

Nearly all involve trading goods and services for advertising, but they could have easily been trades for other goods and services. We hope that after studying these case studies, you step out of your comfort zone and into your creative zone!

The barter-trade examples we are going to present to you are all real deals that were done and are shown to illustrate the incredible leverage that barter trade can give you. Although you may ask, what's the catch? There is none. They were all successful transactions in which everyone won. And all were done with the highest degree of integrity. They are presented to stimulate your mind and imagination with what is possible if you allow yourself to think freely.

CASE STUDY #1: HOW I SAVED A COMPANY FROM BANKRUPTCY, AND THE BIRTH OF RADIO BARTER

My first-ever barter trade happened when I was 27, and it marked the birth of radio barter as we know it. I was offered a job with a public company in the media business. They had just brought a radio station in New Orleans. They sent me to run it. It was a country-and-western station. When I arrived in New Orleans, I found out that they had no money! The sales manager said that they had $0 in the bank, a note of $4,000, and the payroll for $5,000. So I needed to come up with $9,000 in less than thirty days!

 **INSIDE SECRET #55**

Necessity is the mother of invention.

The only thing I had to offer or trade was advertising time at the station, and I had to raise some money fast. So I said to the sales manager, "We need to trade some cars." And he said, "What do you mean?"

He came from the conventional "school of cash." I said, "Let's see if we can trade some cars." Trading was not new; I had heard about people doing trade deals, and so I decided to try it on my station. I knew that car dealers like to trade, so I decided to test the concept.

The sales manager thought the only way that you could sell was for cash! I changed his mindset and paradigm and made him into a "trade salesman." The whole concept of trade had never crossed his mind! It was very simple: we spend the equivalent of money that you spend back with us. Again, $x = y$. You give us \$x worth of cars, and we will give you \$y worth of advertising. And the value of $x = y$.

So I sent him to a local Ford dealer in New Orleans, and they said they agreed to trade three Ford Falcons, which were about \$6,000 apiece (full price, no discounting) for credits to be used for advertising that we would offer them on our radio station in the future. In other words, we would provide \$18,000 in future advertising credits for three Ford Falcons (3 x \$6,000). Remember, I owed \$4,000 for the note and \$5,000 for the payroll. I needed to come up with \$9,000 in less than thirty days. The way to do this was by cash-converting the three cars at \$3,000 apiece. I called a local used-car dealer. I said, "Would you buy three new Ford Falcons for \$9,000?" His reply? "Oh, of course." Normal retail price of these would be \$18,000. So the secondhand dealer was getting 50 percent off the list price and would make a healthy margin reselling them.

So the deal was set to give airtime in the future for three new Ford Falcons. All I had to do was to drive across the river to save the radio station. I was now able to pay the note and make the payroll. Not bad at age 27!

I had to bring three cars back over the bridge to and cash-convert them, but I needed three drivers. It would be myself and the sales manager, and we took Jim, an engineer, as our third driver.

We are at the Ford dealer. I'm all excited because the radio station is going to be saved. The owner of the Ford dealer is in the process of signing the contract, giving us the title to three Ford Falcons, and in return they get $18,000 worth of airtime credit over the next two years. (It was a two-year deal.)

Then suddenly, Jim the engineer says, "Wait a minute." I froze. The owner of the Ford dealer stopped his signature. Jim said, "This doesn't seem fair." I said, "What's the problem?" He said, "You haven't run any advertising for the guy, and he's already giving you the cars."

So I said, "Just a minute. Jim, would you step outside?" And I had to explain to him how barter trade worked. He still did not understand, so I asked him to stand right there. I went back and apologized, the manager of the Ford dealer signed the contract, and we drove the cars back. Then I had a long talk with Jim!

In this deal, I traded 3 cars at $6,000 each for $18,000 in advertising with the Ford dealer. Then I cash-converted the three cars to $9,000 in cash with another local car dealer. This gave me the cash that I needed to cover my cash requirements for the month.

In all barter-trade transactions, everyone wins. The Ford dealer got the advertising they needed to stay in business—and actually ended up cutting its cash advertising costs. I was able to use excess airtime to generate the much-needed cash to cover the note and payroll and provide a living for my employees. The local used-car dealer got three cars at a 50 percent discount.

 **INSIDE SECRET #56**

Anything that is not being used can be put to good use with barter trade. In trade, everyone wins!

Trade became a normal part of business for the station, and we went on to make a profit for ten years to come—with a good portion coming from trade sales, which became a profit center in itself.

And if you are worried about how I handle the tax, I simply reported the $9,000 I got in cash from the cash conversion of the three Falcons on the books as income (or revenue) to the IRS, the way that it should be done.

CASE STUDY #2: HOW I HELPED THE WORLD'S LARGEST CRUISE LINE GET STARTED USING BARTER TRADE

In the early 1970s, I had just moved to Miami, Florida, and I was looking for people to do some trade advertising with. I had heard of a company that had bought a cruise ship called the *Mardi Gras, or Empress of Canada*, which had been owned by the Canadian Pacific company. The ship was a very old ship that had run from Montreal to London.

The ship was in pretty bad shape. But the entrepreneurs who had bought the ship had a whole new vision for cruising.

In the early '70s, cruising was for the newlywed or nearly dead!

The problem was that the owners did not have the money required to fund the complete repairs. The real problem was how to fill the occupancy and berths. They had no cash for advertising, but big dreams!

Now if you are a linear thinker, you would resort to friends, family, or a bank to loan you the money for advertising. Advertising, as we pointed out earlier, is the fuel of a business; without quality advertising, no business can survive or thrive. All businesses need advertising. Word of mouth is simply a form of advertising, and it is not free, as you might think. You earn it by doing a quality job.

The owners of the cruise line needed to fill cabins. My company, WAGI, approached the CEO and made a barter-trade proposition that did not require or involve the use of cash. But it would give them incredible leverage.

The proposition was simple and just required one piece of paper. I told the CEO that I would like to trade the empty berths that they had for media time across the United States. They could select which markets and times. All I wanted was the equivalent dollars in berths or cabins. The ratio of the trade would be 1:1. (We have talked about ratios before. Ratio is what you get compared to what you give.)

The CEO of the cruise line had nothing to lose. They were basically getting no-cash advertising, all by using idle assets that they would be trading at full retail. In other words, if a cabin sold at retail for $1,000 for a one-week cruise, they would get a $1,000 equivalent of advertising at a 1:1 ratio.

We agreed on $500,000 of no-cash advertising per year for the equivalent value of empty cabins on the ship. As part of the agreement, I told them that I would only use the cabins on a space-available basis.

We sat down and decided the markets they wanted to air on, and then I was able to secure ads for them at least 10 times a day in 100 different markets.

So the media plan was 100 different markets or stations, 10 times per day, 365 days per year! The main message was just simply blasting, "Call the Fun Ship. Call the Fun Ship." The message clearly resonated, and people surely called! The cabins started to fill up. The cruise company? It was Carnival Cruise Lines, now the world's largest cruise line, and it all started with a simple barter transaction.

 **INSIDE SECRET #57**

Carnival Cruise Lines got $5 million worth of free or "no-cash" advertising by trading empty and unused cabins at full retail! That is what you call smart business, using out-of-the-box thinking.

They remained a trade client of mine for seven years!

There are a few very important lessons in marketing to be learned here.

Marketing Lesson #1: You need massive advertising to get attention!

Ali explains it best in his book, *Get Your Black Belt in Marketing,* in move #60: you need massive advertising to get attention. It does not matter how good your product is, you need massive advertising to really get attention. People are busy, and they rarely pay attention to what they see in the form of advertising. Like it or not, the most advertised product or service always wins, because these are the ones that come to mind when people need their problem solved. Large companies continue to spend millions of dollars on advertising because it works! And it makes them a lot of money.

Most companies that fail do so because they simply do not have the money to sustain a consistent advertising program to generate a regular flow of qualified leads and prospects into their business.

Brand and brand recognition are the two most important elements of marketing. A brand simply means trust. You trust something either through experience or recognition. The more times you see or hear something, the more legitimate you think it is.

This is why it takes salespeople on average eight to twelve contacts with a prospect before they start to take them seriously. They are simply building their brand awareness, or trust factor, in your eyes.

Tony Robbins' infomercials were aired every thirty minutes somewhere in North America at the peak of his promotion! He understood what it takes to get above and beyond the noise and clutter. Now you know why Tony was called by prime ministers and royalty for coaching and advice. They knew him! He was a brand in his industry!

If you don't think advertising is important, try living without it. No one will know you exist, and no one will notice when you quickly disappear into the dark.

How do I keep my radio stations in business? We simply advertise forty-eight times a day. Yes, that is forty-eight times a day! Or two times every hour. This results in ten leads per week on average from people wanting to advertise on our station.

 **INSIDE SECRET #58**

All smart marketers know that in advertising, the secret formula is: Impact of Advertising = Reach x Frequency.

Reach times frequency means how many people see an ad multiplied by how often they see it. Of course, this assumes that the ad has a good offer. As we explained earlier, advertising never fails. What fails is the offer.

In the case of the cruise line, the reach was determined by selecting radio stations around the country that we thought contained a high population of the target market. This is what marketing folks call demographic analysis. We chose one hundred top demographic markets.

In terms of frequency, the advertisements were on ten times a day on these one hundred key radio stations, with a good offer.

Marketing Lesson #2: You don't need to pay cash for advertising.

Most business owners think that the only way to get advertising is by paying for it. Not true! You can get the most valuable commodity in business (which is advertising) without paying or exchanging any cash. I did not say free; I just said without exchanging cash.

The back end is the bonus!

Most companies make more money on the back end than they do the front end. In fact, companies will even give things away for free on the front end, just to gain the back end revenue. For example, printer companies give printers away and make money on print cartridges; camera folks will give cameras away to make money on film. Blood glucose meters are given away to make money on the strips. I think you get the idea.

 # INSIDE SECRET #59

What barter trade essentially does is give you traffic that you normally would not have.

The trade for the cruise company gave them the traffic that would then spend more money on the gift shops, excursions, and the casinos! This equated to a good chunk of additional revenue.

And soon these trade customers became cash-paying customers and referred others to Carnival Cruise, based on the positive experience they had.

INSIDE SECRET #60

Barter trade gives you the opportunity to get people to experience your business; if they like it, they will come back and refer their friends. It is one of the best marketing tools you have available.

And this definitely worked for Carnival. Within seven years, they did not need to trade; they became a cash-paying customer of mine.

CASE STUDY #3: HOW I HELPED CHRYSLER CUT ITS MARKETING BUDGET BY $21 MILLION

It is December 1972. I get a call from a friend of mine that has an advertising agency in New York. He tells me that he just contacted one of his major clients to wish them a happy Christmas—his client being the marketing director at Chrysler.

But when he called, his client was not celebrating Christmas but was looking over the Michigan Fairgrounds, and all he could see was about 10,000 unsold cars! A marketing director's worst nightmare is always unsold products!

Each car was worth about $12,000 in 1972 dollars at full retail value. So the total market value of the inventory he was staring at was $120 million, just sitting in the snow, collecting dust.

His advertising budget was around $21 million, but this was not enough to move cars at the rate they needed. His advertising budget was not generating enough airtime. Usually car manufacturers sell cars before they make them. But in this case, Chrysler sat with a boatload of cars because of the economic downturn. Of those 10,000 cars, 1,000 were the famous Chrysler Imperials. For those of you old enough to remember, it was the "old boat!"

The Imperials were the real problem. They only did about ten miles per gallon, and with the oil crisis looming, nobody wanted them! They were just not selling. I told my friend that WAGI could trade the 1,000 Imperials that Chrysler was having a huge problem selling for the equivalent in media time: print, radio, or TV. Basically I would coordinate a deal that would give Chrysler five years of advertising credits for the equivalent in cars. In fact, it was better than this: I gave Chrysler a ratio of 2:1 for radio and 1.5:1 for TV. In other words:

Full sticker value of each Imperial = $12,000

Radio credits obtained = $24,000, or a 2:1 ratio

TV and print credits obtained = $18,000, or a 1.5:1 ratio

Considering that these Imperials were something that Chrysler could not sell, it's a very sweet deal for them! And a perfect way of turning a problem into an opportunity!

Chrysler was getting better-than-cash value for their inventory in media time and full sticker price—or nearly twice the advertising for the same dollars! And the reason that they could not move the cars that were actually selling was that they just did not have enough advertising dollars behind them. As we explained earlier, one of the major reasons for business failure is undercapitalization of advertising expenditure.

The ratio of what you give for what you get depends on the desirability of the product or service you are offering. Most of the media stations that I negotiated with thought it was really cool to have an Imperial, and since they had a lot of unsold time, they were happy to give me these ratios. It all depends on what you can negotiate in a trade deal.

Since the media had a lot of capacity, I was able to get some great ratios from them and pass these onto Chrysler. They jumped at the deal, as they did not have to discount the price of the Imperials, they were able to get rid of cars that had sat in the snow for over a year, and they could leverage their purchasing power with these ratios. They had nothing to lose and everything to gain.

The 1,000 Chrysler Imperials equated to $12 million ($12,000 x 1,000). But they were able to trade this for $21 million in advertising (12 x 1.75), because the average ratio was 1.75. WAGI brokered the deal. We did not take control or ownership of any inventory. I just got the brochures of the cars and hit the road, flying across the country to meet all the key media folks. I would fly to a market that Chrysler wanted to advertise in, stay in a hotel, and then call the CEO of the media station to meet me for lunch. I showed them the brochures of the car and asked which color they wanted. I told them that they would be paying for these cars with their unused/unsold airtime, and I told them the ratio I needed. They signed a direct contract with Chrysler for the media credits to be used over five years, but they had to order the cars from me as the broker.

No station is ever 100-percent sold out. So it actually cost them nothing to run the time, and getting 2:1 and 1.5:1 ratios was not an issue.

And they thought the Chrysler Imperials were "terrific!"

Do You Have Any Milk Trucks?

I even made a trip out to Hawaii, where I went to one TV station, the biggest on the big island. And when I offered the owner three Chrysler Imperials for airtime credits, he turned around and said that he did not want them—even though they were essentially free for him. He was the only media station that had turned me down. Why?

He said, "I don't really want Chrysler Imperials, but what I do want is three milk trucks. Do you have three milk trucks?"

I immediately got on the phone to my friend, who called the marketing director of Chrysler and told him the situation: the media

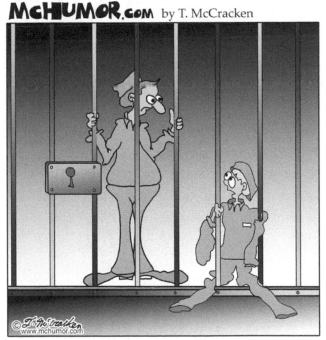

McHUMOR.com by T. McCracken

"Next Father's day I'll buy you
a tie instead of stealing a Ferrari."

station wanted milk trucks, not Chrysler Imperials. His response?

"Oh, just give him what he wants!"

So only in Hawaii did I have to trade milk trucks.

All said and done, I was able to secure $21 million of advertising by travelling across the country and trading cars for media credits with major media stations over a five-year period. This was all done in five weeks. Chrysler had secured $21 million worth of basically free advertising, as it was able to use an asset that was not being used. And using these advertising credits, it was able to sell its complete inventory of the remaining 9,000 vehicles that had been selling slowly.

 **INSIDE SECRET #61**

Once you get good at barter trade, you can take an asset that is not moving and use it to sell other products that are—and cut your advertising budget in the process!

In this case, the asset that was not moving was the old Imperials, and the assets that were moving were the other Chrysler models. In effect, what I was able to do with Chrysler was optimize their marketing spend, by taking something that was lying around collecting dust and using it to cut the marketing expenditures for the existing product line.

If you are wondering how the paperwork happened, it was very simple. The media station was the one with a direct agreement with Chrysler. So each media station signed an agreement with Chrysler to provide airtime in return for advertising credits. This was the so-called scrip.

How Barter Math Truly Makes Magic

In summary, Chrysler had invested in 10,000 cars that were collecting dust and depreciating by the day at the Michigan Fairgrounds. The full market value of these cars was $12,000 per unit in 1972 dollars, or *$120 million*. By using barter trade, Chrysler was able to take a portion of these, the 1,000 Chrysler Imperials that were not moving, and convert them to $21 million in advertising credits by taking advantage of the better-than-cash ratios I was able to obtain.

They essentially traded $4 million worth of cars for $21 million worth of advertising, leveraging their advertising spend by nearly five times and increasing their purchasing power by the same amount.

Summary of the Chrysler Deal

Chrysler Imperials at full retail value:	$12,000
Total asset value of Imperials:	$12,000 x 1,000 = $12,000,000
Chrysler Imperials cost price:	$4,000
Total cost for 1,000 Chrysler Imperials:	$4,000 x 1,000 = $4,000,000
Value of advertising received:	$21,000,000
Leverage gained:	= 21/4 = 5 times!

 # INSIDE SECRET #62

By trading, you immediately multiply your purchasing power significantly!

Chrysler had secured $21 million in advertising for $4 million of hard or invested cost and multiplied its buying power by five times—all with inventory that was in the snow and could not be sold. This is one of the best examples you will see of business optimization and out-of-the-box, creative thinking.

Here Is This Bonus!

Chrysler now took the signed advertising credits it obtained from the media station and was able to get loans to produce more cars, which were now selling as a result of the advertising! The signed advertising credits from the media station were solid collateral to present to the bank. If Chrysler defaulted, the bank could sell these credits (cash-convert them) and get its money back!

Overall, this trade also helped Chrysler's cash-flow problem.

Everyone Wins in Barter!

In barter, everyone wins. Chrysler cut its marketing budget and sold its entire inventory of 10,000 cars, using cars that were collecting snow and depreciating day by day. The media stations were able to sell excess and unused airtime for cars that they wanted—and basically got for free, as they used unsold and unused advertising time. I made a very healthy commission for putting this deal together.

This is a true story of what a little out-of-the-box thinking can do for you. And this same type of deal can just as easily be done in today's economy!

Chrysler was smart enough to look at trade as another avenue to do business, and it paid off handsomely! Remember, trade like cash is just another way of doing business.

It Only Gets Better: The Concept of Better than Free

Ali and I coined the term "BTFT": Better Than Free Trade. In no other business transaction can you actually get BTF. Only a barter trade will allow this. Because:

 # INSIDE SECRET #63

In barter, if you trade with products or services that are going to become obsolete and you to pay to dispose of them, then what you get in return is actually not free, but BTF—Better Than Free!

CASE STUDY #4: HOW THE ROOTS OF THE HOME SHOPPING NETWORK LIE IN BARTER TRADE

Did you know that the Home Shopping Network (HSN) has its roots in a small radio station in Florida that was owned by Lowell "Bud" Paxson? In 1977, due to an advertiser's liquidity problem, the company was paid in can openers by one of its advertisers. The radio station had done a trade or barter in lieu of providing advertising—exactly what we are teaching in this book. No cash, no problem. Bud had about 1,400 can openers in his prize closet. And you now know what a prize closet is. This is a place where radio stations keep items that they might gather by doing various forms of trade deals.

Bud's station was not able to make payroll one day, and Bud needed cash, so he decided to "cash-convert" these 1,400 can openers on the air that were in his prize closet at $9.95 each. In other words, he was converting his inventory to cash by doing a "mini-auction" on the radio.

Since the can openers had been traded for excess/unused airtime on Bud's radio station, the proceeds from the sale were pure profit for him.

The can openers sold out, and Bud made thousands in 1977 dollars—plenty to cover his immediate cash flow problem.

Once Bud had figured out that selling on the air was a good idea, he then began trading and auctioning other goods and services that he had traded for over the radio to the listening audience. Within sixty days, the small Florida station was in the black, and the "seller-on-the air" concept, or "direct marketing," was further tested on the local cable television channel. He then started the Suncoast International Bargainers Club.

Bud had changed the world of marketing by realizing the value of broadcasting as a direct-sales medium back in 1977.

Sensing the sales potential of live, on-air product selling, Bud Paxson and financier Roy Speer cofounded a local cable TV channel (Channel 52 on Vision Cable) in 1982 that sold products directly to Florida viewers, which then launched nationwide in 1985. The channel was the Home Shopping Club, which later became the Home Shopping Network. The company's sales now total several billion dollars a year, and it is valued at several billion dollars.

And it all started with Bud having to cash-convert 1,400 can openers that he had in his prize closet that his station had traded for advertising time!

The radio station later became the new TV network's first-ever home-shopping host and would eventually sell 75,000 different products in over 20,000 hours of live, on-air television. Home Shopping Network stock was one of the fastest-rising stock on the stock exchange. The company went on to change the world of home shopping, and it started by using barter trade.

 # INSIDE SECRET #64

The best form of "seed capital" that you can get in business is to trade what you already have and are not using.

CASE STUDY #5: GOTTA LOVE PINBALL MACHINES

Another simple but fun trade deal I did was with Mattel, the toy company. They had some old pinball machines that they could not sell. I thought they would make a wonderful prize for any TV or radio station. And employees of the radio station would enjoy playing pinball in their spare time.

As we explained earlier, the more desirable the product or service that you have to offer, the more easier it is to trade. Pinball machines seem like a lot of fun; when people get bored, they can start to play.

The value of the 500 pinball machines were about $400 each in 1975, at full retail.

I worked out a trade deal with Mattel in which I would get them the equivalent of advertising for the 500 pinball machines (a 1:1 ratio). I basically traded $200,000 worth of advertising for 500 pinball machines that they could not sell and probably would scrap.

This again resulted in a win/win deal. Mattel won, because they were able to get rid of excess inventory at full retail that they could not normally sell. The media stations won, because they got a few pinball machines that they could play with and have available in their prize closets. Or cash-convert if they wanted.

Mattel did the same thing as Chrysler and used the advertising to promote products that were selling. This way they were able to continue to grow the business during tough economic times.

As you are starting to see, there is a trend here: taking something that has no value, or an idle asset, and trading it for something very valuable that can help you sell your other products and services. This is effective advertising.

CASE STUDY #6: YAMAHA GUITARS

In the early 1970s, Yamaha had 16,000 acoustic guitars that they did not know what to do with. Even way back in the '70s, they were out of fashion as electric ones came in. I made a deal with Yamaha to trade these guitars for $2 million worth of advertising.

I sent letters to every major radio station in America. In return, Yamaha got $2 million worth of advertising credits over two years that they could use to promote any of their products over the air.

The deal worked perfectly. WAGI was successfully able to secure the advertising for Yamaha and convert inventory that really had no value into something Yamaha really needed, which was advertising to sell more of its product lines that were selling or get traffic to keep them in business.

 # INSIDE SECRET #65

Trade equals traffic.

When you use trade correctly, you can generate traffic to your business by trading what you don't need for something you do need—which is advertising, if you are in business. Unless people know you exist, no one will buy from you; advertising is the life-blood of any company.

As you are starting to see, barter trade offers unique benefits at all levels. It certainly is a cash-preservation strategy, but it also can be used to generate traffic to your business.

CASE STUDY #7: HOW TO GET $600,000 WORTH OF ADVERTISING WITHOUT USING CASH

Over the nearly four decades that WAGI has been in barter trade, we have found that most people are not able to see the true power and potential that barter trade has to offer. Why?

 # INSIDE SECRET #66

Because we are so entrenched in cash, barter does not appear on our radar. But if you are able to spot a barter-trade opportunity, you are on your way to becoming very wealthy!

Barter trade can often be the difference between being in or out of business. It can be the deal breaker or the game changer. In this case study, I will show you how I have been able to keep an apartment building in Las Vegas in business for twenty-seven years by getting it $600,000 of advertising without any cash.

It usually takes me time to explain how barter trade works, and even after that, some people get it and some people don't. But I am usually able to get people to give it a try, and when they do, they are blown away with the results, as you will see here.

There was an apartment complex that opened up on the east side of Las Vegas. I approached the owner with the following proposition.

"Give me the two units at the back of the lot, which you have been finding difficult to rent. And I will give you the equivalent advertising credits, or futures."

So if the normal rent was $600 per month, I would give him $1,200 per month in advertising dollars or credits. A simple 1:1 ratio.

Since most people are skeptical when it comes to barter trade, I also told him that if, as a result of the advertising, he was able to fill the apartment completely, I will also give him back his two apartments. Plus, the agreement could be on a month-to-month basis, so as soon as the advertising was able to drive a continual stream of business, our agreement could end.

He had nothing to lose and everything to gain. How could he refuse? So I got control of two apartments in his complex. And I issued a scrip (voucher) for the equivalent amount of advertising dollars and time. The cost of each apartment was about $600 per month ($1,200 per month for both), so he was getting about $14,400 per year in advertising spots for his trade on my stations, based on a 1:1 ratio.

Now normally apartments or hotels in the United States have an occupancy of about 72 percent. Even the best ones rarely rise above 75 percent. The current occupancy was about 20 percent, so I knew even with an extensive media blitz, his apartment complex would only get up to 75 percent. He had 37 apartments, and with my help he probably would only get 28 occupied, leaving 9 always free.

I ran 60-second spots on the radio for them for 5 years! And this was every day, 3 times a day! This would normally have cost them $30,000 per year if they paid cash. But they paid in "trade dollars." As you know now, it does not matter if you pay with trade or cash, you get the same product or service. So they basically got $30,000 worth of advertising per year by trading 2 empty rooms.

And this has been going on for the last 20 years! Unlike Carnival, the motel did not convert to a cash-paying customer, as they did never reach full capacity! I believe they hit the 80-percent mark (a lot higher than the industry norm), which always left about 9 rooms free.

And yes, for the last 20 years, they have always had two apartments free for me. All by trading two rooms that would have always stayed vacant anyway. So those two empty rooms kept them in business! As I told you, barter trade can be the game-changer for many companies, if they are able to see the opportunity. This motel essentially got over $600,000 worth of free advertising over 20 years!

Again, using the barter-trade mindset, they were able to take an idle or dormant asset, which were two empty rooms, and use it to make the apartment complex profitable.

Now you are starting to see a common theme of barter trade: barter is an ideal tool for taking something that is unwanted and unused and converting it into something that is valuable and useful. In this case, again, it was advertising that could keep them in business.

Now, some people will say that you still had to pay the maid and the cleaning service for the two empty rooms. But even if you take $10 a day out for that, you still are getting free advertising and making use of an idle asset to get something useful (advertising) that drives traffic that makes you dollars.

I hope this case study has really opened up your mind to what is really possible, if you set your mind free—which, of course, is the purpose of this book, to start to think creatively.

CASE STUDY #8: CAN I HAVE YOUR TV FOR MY ROLEX?

One of the big questions that always comes up when I explain barter to people is, how do you handle marginability? For example, I may have a TV that has a 20-percent markup. Then I trade with jewelry that may have a much higher markup, like 60 percent?

A jeweler may have a gold Rolex valued at $4,000. And you have a high-definition flat screen TV that is a demo unit that you want to get rid of. But how do you address the issue of marginability— i.e., that his markup is so much more than yours? How do you bring equality to the trade and both win at the same time?

The transaction is shown in an example below:

You agree with the jeweler to give him a flat-screen TV worth $2,000 for $4,000 worth of jewelry. This brings equality to the trade and provides for a win-win because:

1. You end up paying $1,200 for a $4,000 Rolex and save $2,800, on the transaction.

2. The jeweler ends up paying $1,333 for a $2,000 TV and saves $667, on the transaction.

3. Everyone wins!

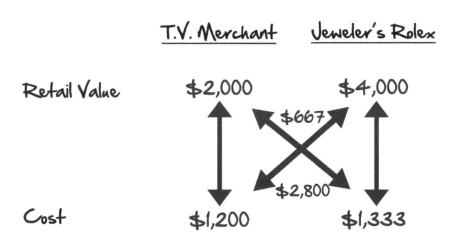

INSIDE SECRET #67

Equality can be brought to a trade situation very easily, and both parties can win. You really can trade whatever you want with whoever you want.

CASE STUDY #9: BATTLE OF THE GIANTS: SHERATON VS. HILTON

For ten years, I had Sheraton Gold as my client. They purchased their media time using trade (trading for rooms), while Hilton paid cash. Guess who came out on top? Sheraton got $5.5 million of advertising by trading what was, in essence, empty rooms. This gave them a very unique advantage at that time in the market.

 **INSIDE SECRET #68**

Barter trade can often be the deal breaker or game changer.

CASE STUDY #10: HOW DHL USED BARTER TO INCREASE ITS MARKET SHARE

Barter is a tool that offers you immense power when used correctly. In this case study, I would like to show you how barter trade can take out your competition.

Several years ago, WAGI had obtained $6 million worth of DHL credits.

Now I had to "cash-convert" the DHL credits to cash. To prevent turbulence in the market, we do not normally trade to customers of people whom we trade with—i.e., we would not sell DHL credit back to their existing accounts.

We asked DHL to give me a list of customers that they had not been able to sell to. Or accounts that they really wanted to penetrate that FedEx had controlled.

They told me about a brokerage house in New York that had been a "long-time" FedEx customer. DHL had no presence here.

They were not able to penetrate this account and really wanted to get access to it.

We approached the brokerage house in New York directly and were able to sell (cash-convert) $300,000 worth of DHL credit.

This example teaches us a very important lesson in barter trade, and that is:

 **INSIDE SECRET #69**

Barter trade allows people to try and experience your business with very little risk or investment. It is the best customer-attraction strategy that exists.

If you are a seasoned business professional, you will know that the hardest part of a business is getting and attracting new customers. If you can get people to try or experience your business, the likelihood is that they, or a percentage of them, will continue to do business with you or refer their friends if they have had a good experience.

In this case, DHL really wanted to get into the brokerage account that FedEx had. Barter trade was the answer, because what they traded with me, I was able to use to get into the account that they wanted.

So barter trade not only provided cash-free advertising for DHL, but also was used as a customer-acquisition tool to break into accounts they could not with conventional cash. DHL and other large companies spend millions of dollars and many years trying to break into major accounts without much success.

So now you have a strategy to go after your competitors' accounts, using barter trade!

CASE STUDY #11: JUST GIVE ME THE DOUGH, MAN!

Most of the case studies you have seen up to now have involved very large companies, some that have even gone on to become billion-dollar enterprises using barter trade. Let's shift gears now and let me show you how barter trade can be applied to an every-day business. We are now going to take a "theoretical" case study. This will cover all the elements of barter trade that you have learned up to now and will clearly show the real-world applica-tion of trade.

The case study is Joe Dough's Pizza Company. Joe owns a pizza company in Miami, Florida. He has been in business for twenty-five years. It is a small little mom-and-pop shop. He does conven-tional marketing, advertises in the yellow pages, and pays $2,000 a month. And he is living "hand to mouth." One day, Joe's baking oven breaks down, which could easily put him out of business unless he repairs it quickly. The problem is that he only has $2,500 in the bank and has used up all his lines of credit. Joe has two choices to get his oven repaired: (1) conventional and (2) creative (out-of-the-box, non-linear barter trade).

Let's study both.

Conventional Approach (Not Recommended!)

Joe can call his friends or look in the yellow pages or online and find oven-repair specialists. He can then decide to go with the guy he trusts or whom his friends recommend. Cost: $5,000. The only problem is that Joe does not have the money. But no cash is no problem! So we recommend that Joe turns to the *unconventional bartering approach!*

Creative Approach Using Barter

Joe has read the book *No Cash? No Problem!* and was taught to always look for ways to conserve cash and maximize cash flow. So he looks in the yellow pages for folks that repair ovens, asks friends, and finally develops a short list of five folks. He calls each for an estimate. They all offer the same price—around $5,000, as was the case with the conventional cash approach. He then offers the one he likes, which we will call Pete's Repairs, the following proposition:

"Pete, of all the vendors I interviewed, I have decided to offer you the opportunity to repair my oven, and I am prepared to pay you your full asking price of $5,000. I am not going to haggle on the price. But in return, I need some flexibility in the way I will be paying you. I will be paying you as follows: $2,500 in cash right now, and $2,500 in pizza vouchers that are fully transferable to anyone you choose and can be used over the next five years at my place of business for food. I assume you eat pizza, and your family or friends will also get to experience my wonderful restaurant!"

Now, what do you think Pete will say? Assuming that he is local, he probably does eat out with his family. And if he does not like pizza, he can always cash-convert the vouchers (sell them to someone else). And if he is doing this work in his spare time, the money he makes from the pizza vouchers is pure profit, and he could get rid of them very quickly if he sells them for fifty cents on the dollar, or 50 percent off!

His hard costs (materials) to repair the oven are probably a lot less than the $2,500 cash that he gets from Joe, and he also gets $2,500 in food vouchers. So all in all, it is a good proposition for him.

But let's look at what happened here a little more closely once they shook hands, and at how thinking creatively and out of the box, and using barter, made no cash no problem for Joe.

After the dust settles, this is what really happens in a barter transaction:

1. *Joe lowered his cost of acquisition about 34 percent.*

Joe paid Pete's Repairs $2,500 cash and $2,500 in vouchers. But the markup on pizza is usually about 300 percent. (This is why you see a pizza store on every street corner!) So the pizza only cost Joe $833. So what Joe "really" paid Pete in currency is $3,333 ($2,500 cash + $833 trade), but in return he gets $5,000 worth of work done! (The higher your margin, the more profitable the trade will become for you, as you are simply trading the profit out of the deal. Trading out your profit is Barter 101, and it is the simplest thing you can do in a barter transaction.) Notice also how it gave Joe an immediate savings of $1,667 on the $5,000 repair, or about 34 percent!

As you see here, by paying $2,500 in "dough" (or pizza), Joe immediately maximized his purchasing power by getting $2,500 worth of plumbing for just $833.

2. *Joe also got what he wanted immediately, but he will not pay for it until Pete orders his first pizza. And Joe got to set the terms of payment with a five-year dating.*

Joe got his oven repaired immediately—which kept him in business, as he had a broken oven! He did not have to go to the bank to borrow the $2,500 that he did not have, or show his balance sheet. If Joe had used cash, he would have had to pay Pete right now—just like when you buy gas for your car, and the money is out of your account immediately after you have finished pumping the gas. Not so good for cash flow! The opposite applies to barter: you don't pay until your product or service is used.

And Joe will not start paying for it until Pete or someone else comes in and redeems the pizza vouchers that Joe gave him and consumes the pizza equivalent to the full voucher amount. Joe gave Pete a five-year dating on the scrip or voucher—i.e., five years to use it. It is highly unlikely that Pete would use all of the scrip in the first year. Basically Joe traded "futures" in terms of pizza meals.

3.   Joe set up a bank in a matter of seconds with zero interest, over the period he wanted!

Joe set up Pete as a bank, Pete basically agreed to finance Joe's purchase and gave a loan of $2,500, and the interest rate was 0 percent. Because Joe set the terms, he got to pay Pete back in the future on a deferred basis and interest free.

4.   Joe keeps the "float."

Until Pete actually uses the $2,500 gift vouchers that Joe gave him, he has the money in his bank and is actually conserving cash. This means he can invest this cash. This concept is called "floating" in the world of barter trade. We've defined this concept already, but we will be discussing it in more detail later on. It is one of the key barter strategies used by barter experts. In barter language, we would say that "Joe has the float until Pete redeems the scrip." More on this shortly.

5.   Joe just developed a mechanism to get people to experience his business, keep them for life, and get referrals!

Joe was very smart, because he is "recycling" his expenditure right back into his business. Some barter experts call this recycled advertising. Pete can only use the gift voucher or scrip at Joe's place of business—nowhere else. So Joe is getting 100 percent return on his advertising dollars. No other marketing vehicle can give you

100 percent return on your advertising dollars. Single-digit returns on your marketing are the norm. Double digits are only achieved by marketing gurus, and triple digits by marketing geniuses. Here Joe issued vouchers for $2,500, and if they are all used, he gets all the money, or 100 percent of the investment recycled back into his business. Nice business, if you can get it. And Joe got it.

It will allow Pete to experience Joe's business, and if he has a good experience, he will probably come back time and time again. So Joe has used barter to acquire a new customer at no cost. And anyone in business knows that the most expensive part of a business is the cost to acquire a new customer!

Now Joe's scrip could be a "rechargeable" card, like those issued these days by most fast-food vendors, so that once the card is finished, Joe could automatically recharge the card for Pete. This way, he would have Pete as a customer for life!

Some may think this is cheeky, but Joe would have to earn the right to do this first by providing an exceptional experience.

The key to business success is to provide people with a quality experience, but you can't do that unless they have the opportunity to try your business. Getting people to "experience you for the first time" is one of the most difficult things to do in a business. It is called "getting customers!"

One of the most powerful but unnoticed marketing strategies known is giving things away for free—i.e., samples, trial offers, etc. But smart marketers know that they are not really giving things away for free, they are simply trading their product or service for your time to evaluate it. Remember, your time is worth something also!

One of the fastest-growing game companies in the UK is a London-based games company called Mediatonic, which gives its games away for free as a mobile application. How can they make money giving away games that they spent money developing? Because 1 percent of the people who download the game and trade their time to play it end up requesting paid customization and upgrades!

One of the keys to a successful business is to get people to experience your business, and the quickest and best way to do this is to trade your product or service for their time through a free offer.

Now, going back to Joe—if he does a good job with Pete and his friends, he will get referrals, which account for the main lead source for most small businesses.

6.   Joe will make 15 to 20 percent on the tips, incidentals, and upsell.

When Pete comes to eat at Joe's restaurant, he will pay a tip on his meal. Tips are usually 15 percent. And that is pure profit to the bottom line. He may order drinks that were not vouchered, and he may decide to order side items, such as salads, that are not vouchered. Joe may upsell him to a dessert that he highly recommends. In fact, all of this is called the "upsell." Each of these will probably add at minimum 15 percent extra profit for Joe Dough's Pizza Company.

7.   Breakage will always work in your favor. It's a fact of life.

There is a 50 percent chance that Pete will not use all of his credits at Joe's pizza restaurant, and maybe a 25 percent chance that he will actually lose the vouchers that Joe gave him. So what happens to these credits? Yes, they go straight to Joe's bottom line. Now Joe hopes that Pete does not lose them—he gave him the vouchers so he would use them—but statistics clearly show that less than

20 percent of people redeem gift vouchers they are given. (Again, this is what barter experts call "breakage.")

Now, when all these seven elements start to add up, they will compound, and Joe will soon find that this is the most profitable purchase he has ever made!

You have seen how replacing cash with creativity changes the whole economics of this deal—and why mindset is what barter trade is all about!

As we move forward, we will be studying more of these types of deals. This was the most basic. But the only thing that is going to change is the complexity, which only depends on the level of imagination you care to have.

 # INSIDE SECRET #70

Every time you trade, you save!

In summary, Joe Dough got what he wanted right now without paying Pete the second $2,500. In other words, he "got the dating." He saved on his acquisition cost and increased his purchasing power by several multiples while paying at a steep discount, and he will pay over a period of time or dating that he decided, interest free—and may even get some breakage if Pete does not use the voucher.

And of course, he gets the float, or the $2,500 that Pete basically loaned him to keep and gain interest on.

And as a bonus, barter will also get Pete and his family to experience Joe's business, and if they like it, they will order drinks and pay a tip and come back, and refer Joe Dough to their friends.

I think we would agree that is very smart.

As for Pete, he got his value of $5,000. He was just paid differently: 50 percent in cash, 50 percent in scrip, and the business that he probably would not have gotten otherwise. Plus he can use or transfer the vouchers he got from Joe to anyone he wants over five years.

They both won!

INSIDE SECRET #71

Barter is all about mutual problem solving. And everyone wins in barter. There is no catch; it is just good business.

Now in this example, Joe did use part cash, but he could have easily traded $5,000 worth of food vouchers, and that would have been a true cashless transaction. But Joe understands that Pete needs some cash to cover his hard costs. So he was only short $2,500 of cash that he was able to trade for.

Again, all this is possible if you were able to use a little creativity and imagination. But if barter is such a smart way to do business, then why don't more people take advantage of it? Because it takes a very different way of thinking, as you have seen, which is something that most people are not accustomed to. And this is why the first chapter of this book was about mindset: changing the way you think and the way you look at a business problem will totally change the outcome. In this very simple example, you can see how very profitable a barter trade becomes if you allow for some non-linear and creative thinking to become part of your life. You can always bring on a third party also. (You will soon see more examples of how this is done.)

Now Here's a Deal You Simply Can't Refuse

A majority of the examples in this book relate to trading advertising for goods and services, because:

 **INSIDE SECRET #72**

In business, the most valuable commodity you can buy (after hiring quality people) is advertising. Advertising is the fuel that keeps businesses going. If your business is successful or unsuccessful, it simply relates to how effective your advertising is. It really is that simple.

All business survive by advertising, whether it's direct using conventional media, or indirect using word of mouth. It is impossible to stay in business without consistent advertising.

If Pete had owned an advertising company, Joe could have given Pete $2,500 worth of advertising for $2,500 worth of pizza. If Joe's business had been in really bad shape, he would seriously need advertising to survive. Pete could start running Joe's ads in the local press tomorrow. Joe would immediately start to see traffic and then make money. But Pete may not consume the pizza for six months at minimum. So Joe probably will have made the $2,500 back before Pete has consumed any pizza.

 **INSIDE SECRET #73**

Barter trade allows you to get what you want right now with trade dollars, which can generate immediate cash for you.

Anything You Can Do, I Can Do Better—but Without Cash!

As you have seen in the simple example above, barter trade can be immensely powerful, and all parties always win. Now if Joe Dough is really short of cash, and his employees ask for a raise, he could even give them vouchers to eat pizza at his restaurant as a form of compensation. Although the employees may already get food for free as part of their compensation, they could easily sell them to their friends who are not already customers of Joe Dough's Pizza Company—yes, cash-convert them.

Alternatively, they could triangulate—i.e., trade the pizza vouchers with a third party to get what they may need or want. For example, they could offer a local garage the pizza vouchers and get their car serviced in return.

In fact, Joe Dough can issue pizza vouchers all day for all types of goods and services he needs to keep their business operational. He is only limited by his imagination!

People Just Don't Think!

As you saw in the Joe Dough's Pizza Company example, if you stop and do the math, you'll find that there was so much more to what appeared to be a very simple trade. In business and in life, I have found that most people just don't take the time to slow down or run the numbers.

Recently I bought a radio station for around $200,000, including the land. I called an assessor and found that the land alone was worth $370,000! This really shows you what a fast-paced and reactive world we live in.

In barter, you need to slow down and run the numbers—and you will soon be amazed at what the potential outcome can be.

CASE STUDY #12: HOW BARTER CAN GET YOU FIRED

The major reasons that people do not use barter are that they either are not aware of it, or they do not understand it. In this case study, I will show you how when the coin drops—i.e, when people get the "aha moment"—they wonder why they were not using it as a business tool before! And they take drastic action as a result.

I had a deal with the Surf hotels in Hawaii. They had six hotels, five of which were doing very well and one that only had a 30 percent occupancy. As you know now, low occupancy and unde-rulitzed assets are all signs of a barter deal waiting to be made. So I told the owners to trade with me and give me rooms at the hotel that was running at 30 percent occupancy, and I would in return give them $1 million worth of advertising. A simple 1:1 trade.

A counteroffer was presented from an advertising agency that offered them $1 million in "pure cash advertising."

The marketing director of the Kona hotel recommended that the CEO go with the agency's all-cash offer. I remember sitting in the meeting. I explained everything to the management team about barter and how it works, as it is laid out in this book. The CEO/owner said that if he went with the agency's cash advertising offer, he would have to pull out his checkbook, and he did not want to write a check. But if he went with my trade advertising offer, he would not have to write a check.

The marketing director wanted him to go with the cash deal rather than trade—and as a result was fired. The CEO figured out that he could get the same advertising by trading empty rooms instead of writing a check!

As a result of this trade, the hotel chain was sold at a high profit!

Business is about economics, and companies should always be looking at ways of saving money. Barter clearly offers any corporation—

small, medium, or large—the opportunity to save and conserve money on their advertising spend, rather than pay cash. It offers cash-free advertising, using assets that are unused and underutilized.

But why is it that most corporations still prefer to purchase their advertising through agencies? Because people making the media buy decision do not have the company's best interest at heart, as this case study showed.

In this case, the marketing director was clearly getting a kickback or commission from the advertising agency for the business, because there is no other reason he should be recommending paying cash for advertising when there is a better, no-cash alternative.

Once the CEO/owner figured out that barter was the optimal way to purchase advertising, he simply fired the marketing director, because he clearly did not have the company's best interest at heart.

 **INSIDE SECRET #74**

If you want to do a real barter deal, you need to get to the person that really cares about the company's bottom line and writes the checks. This is usually the owner, CEO, or CFO.

Remember the story of the pie, when Ali came down to Florida? That's when I taught him Barter 101: Get to the owner of the business first!

This case study clearly demonstrates that barter really needs to be part of your portfolio and modus operandi for business, as it really can save you a lot of money. Don't let anyone convince you differently!

CASE STUDY #13: HOW TO GET A $100,000 MERCEDES AT A 25 PERCENT DISCOUNT

A very well know marketing consultant did some marketing consulting for a Mercedes dealer on the East Coast, but instead of charging them the $5,000 per hour that he usually charges, or $40,000 a day, he asked them to trade or exchange a brand-new $100,000 Mercedes.

The Mercedes cost $100,000, but with rebates, the cost to the dealer was really about $75,000. As we have shown you, anyone can trade the soft costs, or profit, out of a deal. Soft dollars are very easy to trade for something more valuable.

So he ended up trading $75,000 worth of consulting for a $100,000 Mercedes that cost the dealer $75,000. The trade was a 1:1—$75,000 of consulting for the $75,000 hard cost of the Mercedes.

Again, a win-win. The dealer got the consulting that they needed to grow their business, and he got a $100,000 Mercedes at $75,000, or 25 percent off the full-sticker price.

CASE STUDY #14: A PRINTING COMPANY WITH IDLE TIME

A printing company in California figured out the concept of barter and put it to very good use. They had two hours out of their eight-hour day that the machines and personnel in the printing shop were actually doing nothing, or were idle. Yes, for two hours per day, both the machine and people were sitting doing nothing! Although the two hours were idle, all the fixed costs were covered—i.e., rent, electric, etc.

So any extra utility would basically be pure profit. The printing company worked out a trade. They talked with a local radio station and offered them the opportunity to print some collateral flyers in return for airtime.

They designed and printed $1,000 flyers for them. Their out-of-pocket expenses were only the cost of the raw materials (i.e., ink and paper); the personnel and machine time were already covered as part of the fixed overhead.

The cost of the ink and paper was negligible at around $100. They traded at 1:1 at full retail—i.e., they got $1,000 worth of advertising for $1,000 worth of printing.

Since the printing was done using excess capacity in spare and unused time that was essentially paid for, what they got in return was essentially free—and the best example of business optimization and out-of-the-box thinking you will see.

The math is as follows:

Advertising credit:	$1,000
Paid with printing:	$1,000
Cost of printing:	$100
Leverage:	10 times!

The printing company was able to get $1,000 worth of printing for $100, or a leverage of 10 times!

The printing company continues to be very profitable, because it understands leverage.

CASE STUDY #15: PAY THOSE UNWANTED VENDORS WITH TRADE DOLLARS

As you have seen by now, trade is the same as cash—the only difference is that you don't pay in cash. But you have the same rights and privileges as if you paid with cash. In a trade deal, you pay in "trade dollars," or with the items that you want to trade.

I went to a hotel in Las Vegas, and I asked them how many vendors they had. They said that they had about 400. I told them that I could save them money by simply converting a portion of these vendors from cash to trade. In other words, they could pay the vendors in vouchers to stay at the hotel and immediately save on their accounts payable. I worked with the hotel and saved them a significant amount of money on their accounts payable.

You need to get in the mindset that a trade dollar is equivalent to a cash dollar, and it offers you the same rights and privileges.

CASE STUDY #16: A PROFESSIONAL PRACTICE CAN MAKE USE OF THOSE FEW EXTRA HOURS

If you are a independent professional, maybe a doctor, dentist, chiropractor, or optician, you may have an hour or two available in your daily schedule. You can trade that valuable hour for something that you may want or need. How? By finding someone that has what you need and trading with them directly or through a trade club.

I know many independent professionals that take advantage of this mindset. Some trade clubs have up to 24,000 members, so there are plenty of "goodies," or goods and services, that you may choose from. Stay tuned—we will cover trade clubs in the next chapter.

CASE STUDY #17: JUST TELL ME WHAT YOU WANT; I CAN GET IT

In the early 1970s, I bought a radio station in Carmel, California. It was an old station and needed some engineering work done. I was already trained in the barter mindset and knew that the best way to source products without using cash is to use barter. As you now know, it saves a lot of money on acquisition cost and leverages your purchasing power immensely. So I decided to put a trade deal together. I told the engineering contractor that I would not be able to pay him in cash and asked him if I could trade with him for something he may need instead. So I simply asked him what he really needed, or something that he would be paying cash for in the next thirty days.

He said that his wife was looking for some breast implants. And he really needed these to keep his relationship with his wife!

Now, remember what the great Zig Ziglar said: "For you to get what you want in life, you need to help others get what they want first."

So for me to get the engineering work that I needed, I just needed to find someone who would do breast implants on trade. I went through my client list for the radio stations and found that I had a plastic surgeon in San Jose for whom I had previously advertised. So I called him and told him that I had another client who needed breast implants for his wife, and provided advertising for the plastic surgeon that allowed me to complete the transaction. The plastic surgeon was happy to do the trade, as he had more to gain than to lose. And when the dust settled, what transpired was that the engineering contractor's wife got the breast implants; I got the engineering work I needed; and the plastic surgeon got the additional advertising on my radio station. And no money changed hands. No cash, no problem! Everyone wins in barter!

We all basically traded our excess time, and we benefited and profited! It did not cost the plastic surgeon any more time, as he did the surgery in his excess capacity. It did not cost my radio station anything, as I had unsold airtime. And it did not cost the engineering company anything, as they were not running at full capacity either. So we triangulated—i.e., had three parties in the deal—and we all benefited!

Barter works perfectly when everyone has excess capacity.

We hope by now that you are starting to adopt the barter mindset, and see that:

INSIDE SECRET #75

When you trade, you will always save, as you are in most cases gaining extra utility from something that is surplus and with something that you have already paid for!

CASE STUDY #18: A FEW WORDS CHANGE EVERYTHING IN BUSINESS AND LIFE

However hard I try, some people will never understand barter trade, as you saw in the Mazda deal ("we don't trade"). Yet they agreed to the deal when I told them that I was buying the cars and paying in advertising dollars.

In the same way, one of my best salesmen came up with a "can't say no" proposition for barter. He was a trade salesperson. In my stations, we have both trade and cash salespeople.

The cash salespeople bring in cash business for advertising space. The trade folks bring in trade or "goodies" for the prize closet, which we either keep, give to friends and clients of the radio station, or maybe cash-convert.

Why was he so good at trade, and my number-one trade salesperson? Because what he did was very simple—he just phrased the barter-trade proposition in a way that you could not say no to. He went to a local furniture store and said:

"For every dollar you spend with me on advertising, I will buy the equivalent amount of furniture in your store. How much furniture would you like me to buy?"

Now that is an offer that you cannot refuse at face value. It may really simply be a trade proposition, but because he used the word "buy," like I did with the Mazda folks, it changed the whole dynamics of the transaction. The furniture store thinks that he is able to sell some furniture, and everyone's business needs to sell more of what they have.

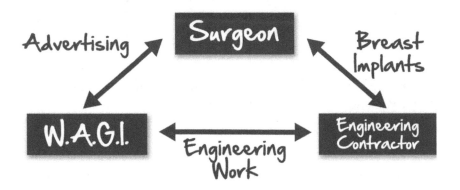

We ended up trading $50,000 worth of furniture in his store for $50,000 worth of airtime on my station. And since the airtime cost me nothing, it was an unused asset, so I was able to do it at zero cost.

I then turned around and cash-liquidated the $50,000 worth of furniture at a discount.

I hope from this chapter you have learned different ways to put together creative deals. These are all real examples of real deals, or case studies, to spark your mind and imagination. Are you now ready to do your first trade deal? If you are still nervous about going alone, maybe you need to join a trade club. Read on!

THINGS TO REMEMBER FROM THIS CHAPTER

- Everyone trades; now it's your turn to start!
- You get the same rights and privileges with trade as with cash.

- Your biggest breakthroughs will always happen when you think out of the box.

- If you are in business, you need advertising—it is your fuel. Without it, your business will simply stop.

- Barter trade allows extra utility from something that you have already paid for.

- You must get to the decision maker—the owner, CEO, or CFO—to make a trade deal!

chapter seven

—— 7 ——

Will You Join My Club?

I don't care to belong to a club that accepts people
like me as members.

Groucho Marx

One of the biggest questions that we get is, where do I find people to trade with? Most of the deals and case studies that you have read about so far have been about me trading 1:1, or maybe me brokering a deal.

But barter has evolved to a highly sophisticated form of commerce with the emergence of trade clubs. These clubs allow members to obtain virtually anything they would normally pay cash for, but in exchange for their goods or services.

At any reputable trade club, you can get access to clothing, auto services, toys, food, home repairs, medical services, dental services, entertainment, lodging, construction, ski services, beauty services, health, computers, business services, recreation, vacations, advertising, tires, dentists, optometrists, and vacation rentals. Or basically anything you need and would normally pay cash for.

These clubs are where you find people who are just like you and are anxious to trade with you!

Trade clubs take you back to the good old days, when people simply traded with people. Here you meet like-minded folks who understand the advantage of using trade to supplement cash income and to generate a profit center.

FOUR REASONS TO JOIN A TRADE CLUB

1.   *You get what you want without reaching for your wallet or checkbook.*

Trade clubs are an "outlet" for you to dispose of your excess inventory, capacity, or skills to other members of the club. Most trade clubs operate like banks in their own right, issuing their own currency.

Basically a trade dollar is equivalent to a US dollar. When you do some work or sell something to someone in the club, your account is credited with the equivalent in trade dollars. Trade dollars are only redeemable with members of the club.

In fact, many clubs will issue you a plastic card, just like a Visa card, and this can be used at places that display the trade club's logo (i.e., who are members of the club).

As you can see, this is identical to using your plastic credit card, but you are paying with goods and services, not cash!

 **INSIDE SECRET #76**

You need to think of a barter-trade transaction as identical to a credit or cash transaction. You can even use a plastic credit card to pay, but you are not paying cash, you are paying with your goods or services!

And just like banks, trade clubs will send you a monthly statement of your credits and debits, and you can view your balances online.

2.   You gain access to new channels.

One of the key advantages of a trade club is immediate access to a set of well-qualified buyers—people eager and anxious to trade with you. When you join a trade club, you are normally asked to develop a profile of your product, service, or offering, and you are assigned an account representative. This person will then market your product or service to other members of the club.

 # INSIDE SECRET #77

Joining a professional trade club will give you access to a whole new marketplace of people who are interested to learn about what you have to offer.

 # INSIDE SECRET #78

Commercial trade clubs focus on driving new business to existing businesses.

When you do work for someone in a trade club, you "bank credit" in that club that become trade dollars you can draw on or use to purchase other goods from other members.

The simplest way to think about trade is just like cash, as we continue to point out in the book—the only difference is that you are not paying hard cash or dollars!

3.   All the paperwork is done for you.

Unless you are a member, you cannot gain access to the private directory listing who else is in the club. And the trade club also handles all the paperwork for the transactions that you make, which includes providing you with the correct tax documentation at the end of the year. Since 1982, the IRS has had very defined laws on the way barter transactions needed to be accounted for.

All your account information is online with a full customer-service facility, 24/7, for payment processing and billing, just like a bank—which is basically what they are.

4.   Trade clubs can be used for both business and pleasure.

Trade clubs are not just for businesses, but also for individuals who are looking to trade. You don't have to be a full-fledged legal business to join a trade club. And now that you have seen the advantage of trade, you will want to consider using it for both business and pleasure. And to get rid of those items you may have in your garage!

I WILL GIVE YOU SOME OF MINE, IF YOU GIVE ME SOME OF YOURS!

Trade exchange clubs have been around for thirty years. They are primarily a B2B marketplace for cashless transactions.

There are other places where you can do what people call commercial swaps, like craigslist. But commercial exchanges are much more formal and focus on business to business. You can basically swap, barter, or trade with anyone else in the club or community.

WELCOME TO THE FOURTH TRANSACTION VEHICLE!

By now, we hope that you have come to the conclusion that barter trade is identical to cash; the only difference is that you do not pay with cash. Sorry to sound like a broken record!

Trade clubs simply provide a cashless marketplace for trade to occur.

MCHUMOR.com by T. McCracken

"Under 'associations' you belong to you
listed The Zowie Monster Movie Video Club.
Any others?"

INSIDE SECRET #79

Trade clubs could be considered to be in direct competition with cash, check, and plastic.

They offer another form of payment within the club, which is their goods and services.

Trade clubs are now on the comeback, as more and more individuals and businesses are finding they have excess time and inventory on their hands. They offer the perfect outlet and immediate access to an active marketplace.

Although trade clubs are a now a fourth transaction vehicle, they need to be kept in perspective. Trade clubs will probably never replace the other alternative currencies (cash, check, or plastic), because of the convenience factor. And they were never meant to.

 **INSIDE SECRET #80**

Trade clubs are just an alternative tool to cash, checks, and plastic.

In the barter world, you will hear the word "private currency." Each exchange has its own currency that can only be used within the exchange and with the members, and not in public markets.

But trade exchanges offer an excellent channel and community in which to trade products, goods, or services that you cannot sell for cash, while allowing you to conserve cash.

WORKING WITH TRADE CLUBS

We understand that it can be daunting to approach a trade club for the first time, but they are the best way to cut your teeth into the world of barter trade. Just by joining a club, you get educated in the whole process of barter trade and get to talk with like-minded people. With people holding your hand.

There are many types of barter clubs. Some may be franchised or independent, nonprofit or profit-oriented, business-oriented or social-service-oriented, informal or highly structured, etc. The details vary from one club to the next.

There are many trade clubs. You can even get a list by going to NATE, the National Association of Trade Exchanges.

Joining a club requires some paperwork, and they will require your tax ID to ensure that your taxes are correctly accounted for. Some may do a credit check and ask for personal details. This is just to ensure that you deliver on your promise, as trade is all about honoring credit.

Each trade club will have its own fee structure; some will charge you a small monthly fee to handle your accounts and website, and a percentage fee on all your transactions. Some may have a sign-up fee.

It is always a good example to ask the trade club if you can talk to club members about their experiences.

 **INSIDE SECRET #81**

Think of trade clubs like the yellow pages. They have a full list of members that are willing to do business with you on trade.

It is always best to contact the Better Business Bureau (BBB). The BBB might have a record of complaints against the barter club or exchange.

The following three steps should help you when working with trade clubs.

1. Be certain that the members have the goods and services that you need. (Judge the credibility and professionalism of the club's brochures and newsletters.)

2. Consider the age and size of the club. Find out the years of operation and total trading volume.

3. Talk to some members. Ask for a members list and call some yourself.

Trade clubs are the shortcut; they simply eliminate the need to find people who think like you and would like to do business like you—i.e., prefer to trade rather than pay cash! In these clubs, you will find some of the smartest business people in the world and very successful businesses. Nearly all the major media in the United States are members of some trade club. Club membership also includes major hotel chains, major league football franchises, other major franchises, etc. You would really be surprised to see who is in the club, and you would immediately recognize the businesses as people you know or would like to do business with. But for confidentiality reasons, we cannot publish the names of people who are members of trade clubs.

Nearly every type of product or service imaginable is part of a trade club. And trade clubs are associated with other trade clubs around the world, which means if you join a respectable trade club, you could be a dentist in Walnut Creek, California, who does work for a lawyer in San Francisco, California. The lawyer's trade account is debited and your account is credited with "funny money" or "private currency," and now you have x barter bucks or credits to spend with anyone in the club! You could use them to stay at a hotel in Sydney, Australia, should they be a member of the trade club network. The trade club system would handle the accounting, booking, etc. Very powerful!

So now you are seeing how trade clubs work. It is not complex. It is simply like-minded people working with like-minded people. It is a network of people who trade with each other, with the club keeping the records. Each gains equivalent value, and it eliminates the need to try to find people who have the barter-trade mindset. Do visit natebarter.com or irta.com before you join an exchange.

TRADE CLUBS OFFER QUICK LEVERAGE

Jake Kaestner wanted his five-person landscaping company to grow, but he didn't have much money to invest in the business. After hearing about a national barter exchange, Kaestner, founder of Kaestner Lawn Care in St. Peters, MO, gave it a try. On barter exchanges, members earn barter dollars by doing work for each other. So Kaestner's $500,000 company did about $4,000 worth of landscaping at the home of another exchange member, a massage therapist. Kaestner turned around and used those barter dollars—currency good only between members of the exchange— to buy advertising in a local paper. "I didn't do any advertising before because it gets expensive," he said. Kaestner has since used barter dollars to buy advertising in local magazines, newspapers, and coupon books. He says those ads are a big reason revenues increased 30 percent that year.

Source: Amy Barrett, "Using Barter to Grow," *Bloomberg Businessweek*, April 16, 2008.

One of the most overlooked but valued opportunities that business people miss out on is how to leverage trade clubs to build your business.

Remember that a trade club is simply a marketing organization. They will send out e-mails and call other members to tell them about your product or service.

If you do an outstanding job with another trade club member, they will not only continue to do business with you on trade, but they may do business with you on cash, or refer you to cash-paying customers.

 # INSIDE SECRET #82

If you join a large trade club, you will have immediate access to about 22,000 prospects. How much would it cost you to get a list of 22,000 well-qualified prospects? Plus all the referrals if you do a good job! And maybe cash business also!

Again, this all takes a different mindset. Think what is possible when you think of trade.

AMERICAN EXPRESS: THAT WILL DO NICELY!

When plastic credit cards were introduced in the mid-1980s, there was a lot of misunderstanding, resistance, and even confusion. It was a new form of currency—the third form of currency, after cash and checks. We were not used to using plastic. How could plastic represent money?

But today you would not leave home without it, as American Express would say. Plastic credit and debit cards are now more used than cash itself. So we are living in a cashless society already. But the plastic represents cash, and your payment is ultimately in cash.

All major retailers have American Express, MasterCard, or Visa signs showing you that they accept these cards as a form of payment.

In the same way, any business that offers trade will also have a sign in its window showing that it takes trade credit as a form of payment. So trade as the fourth form of payment is quickly catching on! And it is backed by your product and services.

Barter trade clubs have a lot of potential. They are estimated to have only captured less than one-half of 1 percent of the market.

But as cash becomes short and inventory rises, you will continue to see this number rise rapidly.

DO BUSINESS LOCALLY, GROW GLOBALLY

One of the keys to business success is networking, and the same applies to barter trade. Although a large national trade club may have up to 22,000 members in the United States, they would be networked with other trade clubs across the world, and so by joining your local trade club, you would have access to 200,000 members across the world!

"I never leave home without my American Express card."

EXCESS CAPACITY EXCHANGES

Besides local and national barter-trade clubs, there are also some major exchanges that specifically focus on excess capacity. Two are worth mentioning.

Active International is the world's biggest corporate barter company. They operate in thirteen countries and do about $1.4 billion in trade. They usually deal with desperate companies. Instead of money, Active gives companies barter credits for last season's clothes, spare hotel rooms, or tins of peas, which they can swap for goods and services they need at a later date. A common purchase with the credits is advertising, company travel, or printing, bought at a discount through Active's trading desks. You may have a large amount of products you need to move; instead of selling it off at a discount or cents on the dollar, you will get the full value, but in credit.

Another major global player is BarterCard International, originally from Australia but now based in thirteen countries with 2,000 participating businesses in the UK alone.

THINGS TO REMEMBER FROM THIS CHAPTER

- To trade, you need more than one person. This is why trade clubs were established—to help you find barter partners.
- Trade clubs are simply marketing organizations.
- Trade clubs solve the problem of finding people to trade with.
- Always review the members list of any trade club before you join.

- A trade clubs can have several thousands of members and can be networked to other trade clubs around the world.

chapter eight

8

The 15 Key Bartering Strategies Summarized

The essence of strategy is choosing what not to do.

Michael E. Porter

We have shared numerous case studies and examples with you to show you the power and potential of barter trade. These were all real-world case studies, or examples of how barter was or could be used to gain immense leverage.

To help you understand how all of these may apply to you, we have summarized what barter trade can do for you into fifteen key strategies. Any one of the strategies below, when implemented and executed in your business and life, will provide you with an immense competitive advantage.

Please take the time to study each strategy, and see how you can use it in both your business and personal life.

1. Lower the cost of acquisition on your purchases.

As you have seen, whenever you trade, you save, because the cost is based on the cost of supplying the goods and services, while you are trading at full retail. So barter trade really is the quickest and easiest way to leverage your purchasing power.

The longer the dating on the scrip, the less you pay, which is the reverse of cash. So the longer you make the scrip, the less you will end up paying. Interest free, of course!

MCHUMOR.com by T. McCracken

2. If you become really good at trading, you can compound your leverage with ratios.

Barter trade on its own is an immensely powerful tool to gain leverage. But it only gets better: the more desirable your product or service is, the more opportunity you have to gain leverage. This is done in terms of ratios.

As you have seen, most trade is 1:1. This is $x = y$, or fair trade. But if you have a very desirable product, you can often get more than what you give.

It is not uncommon for car trade deals to get many more times the value in advertising than the value of the vehicles.

I (Dave) have done deals and also negotiated deals where I have given people a 2:1 ratio—i.e., twice as much advertising versus the value of goods and services that they were trading. Why? Because the goods and services were so highly desirable.

3. Barter equals sales.

We hope that if you have learned nothing else from this book, you have learned that barter trade is a sale, just like any other sale. You just don't pay or receive cash for it. For it to be a true cashless transaction, no cash can trade hands.

What occurs in a trade sale is a transfer of ownership of goods or services from one person to another.

So barter trade is able to increase your sales, without using any cash.

4. Barter can be used to pay operating expenditures. Even payroll!

If you really start to think of your goods and services as currency, then you should be able to do anything that you would normally do with currency, right?

If you are a business, one of the biggest challenges you have is cash-flow management. Since barter does not use cash, it is (or should be) your CFO's best friend. You have seen how I pay most or nearly all my vendors using barter trade, and that includes the janitor, gardener, dry cleaner, attorney, etc.

I even use it to pay my employees: most of my employees are part cash, part trade. Any company can cut its vendor expenses by at least 50 percent if it decided to trade with them instead of pay them cash.

5.   *You can print your own currency.*

The barter person's currency is called the scrip. It is legal tender, but it is only redeemable at your place of business. By issuing a scrip, you are no longer at the mercy of your bank. You now truly have unlimited purchasing power, as long as you can fulfill on the trade.

Having your own currency allows you to afford things that you previously could not afford on a cash-paying basis.

We would highly recommend that you immediately print up and start using your own currency; this will allow you to get what you want right now, and only pay when someone comes in to redeem the scrip you issued, or part of the scrip at sometime in the future.

6.   *Get better terms, credit, and discounts than you ever could by paying cash.*

You have seen in the case studies how barter gives you better terms than cash, because you set the terms, and you never actually exchange any cash.

Let's say you agree to give $5,000 credit to a printer, and he gives you $5,000 worth of printing and delivers it—immediately. You now issue barter scrip, or credits, that give the printer one to two years to use his credit with you. But until the printer actually uses those credits, you haven't paid out a thing. And since he probably will only use a smaller portion of his credit with you at a time, its cost will be easily handled a little at a time as opposed to all at once.

The longer he takes to use your credits, the less it is really costing you. The whole transaction is also based on terms and conditions that you set.

7.   *Understand the concept of breakage.*

Breakage, as you have seen, goes straight to your bottom line in a trade deal. It is basically the unused portion of your barter scrip or voucher. The only real difference between a gift card and scrip, as you now know, is that a scrip has associated with it very specific terms of conditions and usually a expiration date.

You saw the example of the hotel that I traded with in New Orleans. I issued a scrip with them for $125,000 worth of radio and TV time with a one-year expiration date for the equivalent of rooms, or a 1:1 trade.

The hotel immediately got $125,000 in advertising at regular cash rates. This was advertising that they had been paying cash for.

But at the end of the twelve months, an audit revealed that only $35,000 of the $125,000 barter scrip that I had issued had been used for rooms. The rest, or $90,000, had gone unused!

The actual cash cost of the hotel delivering $35,000 worth of rooms was only $5,000. The hotel had basically leveraged up $125,000 in advertising for $5,000.

However, this doesn't take into consideration two overlooked (but extremely significant) other factors.

- Statistically, $35,000 in room trade produces $17,500 in food, beverage, and miscellaneous cash sales, with a gross profit in excess of $8,000 for the hotel. So when all the dust settles, the hotel actually got paid $3,000 net after all costs to enter into this trade ($8,000 profit less $5,000 cost to fulfill on the $35,000 worth of rooms). This is what we call better than free (BTF)!

- All $35,000 worth of rooms were not used at one time. It was spread out over twelve months, meaning that hotel got to pay the $5,000 over twelve months totally interest free. In essence, they got $125,000 worth of advertising up front and got paid to do so.

Most people who are new to barter trade will miss the concept of breakage. But just like ratios, breakage continues to add and compound leverage to the barter transaction.

As we pointed out earlier, breakage is not meant to be manipulative; it is a truism and a fact that people will never use the full scrip. But you always need to stand behind and honor the transaction.

8. Master cash conversion strategies.

Your barter trades will mean that you will end up with "goodies" or items that you either need or want—or may need to dispose of. Most media stations have what we call "prize" closets. These are simply the storage of items they have acquired by trading excess airtime.

Although you think when you watch TV, read a newspaper, or listen to a radio station that they are running at full capacity, this is not true. Media stations are a business just like any other business. And no business runs at full capacity. This is why the media has salespeople to sell advertising space.

Barter trade can be used in multiple ways. You usually use it to acquire things that you need and want by exchanging items that other people need and want in return.

In many cases, the media has so much excess capacity that they must exchange their excess capacity for things that they may later cash-convert.

As we have said before:

 **INSIDE SECRET #83**

Cash is king, but barter is a great tool to get it!

Cash will always be king because of its universality and convenience. Cash transactions are instantaneous and require no education.

 # INSIDE SECRET #84

Because we are so deeply entrenched in the cash system, we have actually forgotten how to do barter-trade! We need to be reminded!

Barter takes education and takes time, but it is one of the most powerful leverage-creation tools you will ever encounter.

When you become good at bartertrade, you will:

1. Be able to save cash, since you are not using it!

2. Generate cash through cash conversions.

3. Continue to generate cash through investments.

Any items that you acquire as a result of a trade can be cash-converted (i.e., converted to cash). In the case of the media, they will simply sell the item to friends and clients of the media, or within their own network at a discount. Or at a fee well above the cost of acquiring them—which in most case is $0, if they are trading advertising space that would normally go unsold or unused and thus would have produced zero revenue unless it was traded.

Barter trade can very quickly solve your cash problem, because it does not use cash but actually generates cash through cash conversions.

And finally, barter is one of the best ways to get people to experience your business, and should they like it, they will continue to patronize it and convert to long-term, cash-paying customers. Carnival Cruise Lines was a trade customer for seven years before it went to cash. This is what we call "cash-continuation."

9.   Create a barter profit center.

Most companies have salespeople, but these are for cash only. As you saw in my first barter-trade deal, once I was able to save the New Orleans media station from bankruptcy using barter-trade, I realized that barter-trade could in itself be a profit center.

The profit center can be created in numerous ways. Some people who are not effective in cash selling are extremely successful in bartering.

For example, a prominent travel magazine traded airline credit for full pages of advertising in their magazine. One page sells for $15,000, so they receive $15,000 worth of first-class tickets every time they run an ad.

The actual hard-cost of the page of advertising to the magazine is a mere $750, or one twentieth the rate they are charging.

The magazine set up a barter liquidation department to cash-convert the credits ASAP for cash flow. The department took the airline credits and immediately resold the tickets for eighty cents on the dollar (twenty cents less than anyone could buy the tickets for directly from the airline itself). The barter profit center basically took magazine ad pages that cost them $750 and turned them into $12,000 of revenue.

Now you can see how easily a company can set up its own barter profit center.

Does this give you any ideas of ways you could profit from operating a barter profit center of your own, inside or outside your business? With a barter profit center, you can net profits of double or quadruple your costs in a few weeks.

I have seen companies where the income of the barter profit center dwarfs other divisions.

10. Leverage your available advertising budget exponentially!

You have seen in nearly all of the case studies how I have traded advertising for different products and services. How ratios simply compound the leverage power for companies. And how companies like the Home Shopping Network and Carnival Cruise Line all became giants by understanding and mastering this one strategy.

If you learn nothing else from this book but how to leverage your advertising spend using barter trade, our time and effort will have been well invested.

In a business situation, using items that have no or little value to you and being able to trade them or leverage them for something that is really very valuable (i.e., advertising) is one of the smartest things you can do. It simply gives you an exponential and unlimited advertising budget.

I showed how I traded with DHL and was able to penetrate an existing FedEx customer using barter trade—and how that customer eventually became a cash-paying customer for DHL. That account has remained with DHL for about eight years and is estimated to do about $3 million per year. So that one single barter-trade transaction was worth, in my estimation, about $24 million.

What kind of advertising budget would you need to generate $24 million worth of revenue?

11. Finance rapid growth without cash.

The best example of this is the Carnival Cruise Lines case study, now the largest cruise line in the world. You saw that they started with one ship and insufficient operating capital. They traded empty cabins with me for radio, television, and newspaper advertising in one hundred cities over a seven-year period. The cost of an empty cabin once the ship sails is minimal. Plus the passengers may spend considerable cash in the bar, casino, gift shop, and shore excursions; thus the net cost to the cruise line to fill an empty cabin was literally less than zero. They clearly understood financial leverage and how to finance rapid growth without the use of cash to become the largest cruise line in the world. They made a massive profit off the bartered cabin being occupied instead of going out empty.

I continuously advertised for them in one hundred cities for more than seven years without them spending a penny of hard cash.

I would conservatively estimate of the amount of sales that the advertising generated was was $100,000,000. It made the founder a billionaire. And it all started with one thirty-year-old ship, no cash, and some creative thinking!

12. Barter is a perfect vehicle to continually generate cash rather than sell at closeout.

Once I helped a cosmetic company. We traded a deodorant line that was no longer being manufactured. It was basically leftover inventory that would have made its way down the food chain to discount outlets.

I gave them the full equivalent of advertising credits for their deodorants, thus getting them full market price in value for undesirable items (items that were now out of style).

The advertising was used to advertise a new line for the cosmetics company. The old goods, which probably would have only brought in ten cents on the dollar as a close-out item, brought full market value as an advertising trade; thus the chief financial officer did not have to "write down" the product. The company was saved not only the book loss, but the cash loss too!

In summary, they were able to take an item that was destined for the closeout or discount market and benefit from it at full price, while also saving millions of dollars in cash.

13. Turn excess inventory into cash without losing regular business.

I worked with a major international hotel corporation that issues its own barter certificates in the amount of $7,000,000 per year. The certificates over the years have become extremely popular in the advertising community, since they are used at more than 1,500 hotels around the world. The hotel corporation is able to trade for advertising on nearly any radio, TV, or outdoor advertising company on a trade basis because of the popularity and desirability of their hotels, which have developed over the years. An estimated $10,000,000 a year in cash is saved through this process by the hotel corporation. And all as incremental business.

14. Recycle dollars right back to your own pockets.

Using barter trade is the best way to recycle dollars straight back into your business. Have you noticed when you go to return a product, they will always offer you store credit to ensure that the refunded dollars are spent back at their place of business?

In the same way, by issuing scrip, you are locking people into doing business at your place of business, as the scrip is not redeemable at any other place of business.

In the City of Palm Springs case study, they required that the media redeem its credits only in Palm Springs' places of business, thus bringing back the money that it spent on advertising right back to the City of Palm Springs, so they could collect the taxes. And the entire multi-million dollar budget was 100-percent recycled back into the hands and bank accounts of Palm Springs merchants.

The tourist bureau didn't care if a magazine bought a car, stayed at a hotel, booked travel through a travel agent, or ordered furniture from a furniture store—so long as they did it with a Palm Springs merchant.

If you are a business that is spending $1,000 per month on advertising, you might as well print $1,000 gift vouchers and give them out to people on the street. A $1,000-per-month ad in the yellow pages probably brings in only a 2 to 3 percent response rate.

Alternatively, if you give out $1,000 worth of gift vouchers, you only pay for those that are redeemed! That is pay-per-business, not pay-per-lead advertising!

15. Use barter to provide stockholder benefits.

Nearly all corporations are doing some form of barter, as they are trading their employees' time for money. A lot of media stations will provide employee benefits, cars, vouchers—all that they have received from some form of barter-trade.

THINGS TO REMEMBER FROM THIS CHAPTER

- There are fifteen key barter-trade strategies. Each on its own is immensely powerful, but working together they compound to give you incredible leverage.

PART 3:
Doing Your First Deal

chapter nine

— 9 —

Time to Hand Over Your Wallet!

A man is usually more careful of his money than he is of his principles.

Ralph Waldo Emerson

Although you may think this book is about barter or trade, it is really about challenging you to think creatively and outside the box. We really do believe that mindset is more important than method. Once you get into the barter-trade mindset, the deals will come automatically. The purpose of this book is to open your mind and imagination to what is possible if you allow yourself to think creatively and, in many cases, out of your conventional comfort zone. We want to condition you to believe that lack of cash does not have to be a show-stopper or an excuse for you anymore. Using trade, you can do exactly the same as you would with cash—and as you have seen in the case studies, a whole lot more. As the title or promise of this book points out, no cash really is no problem, because you can use your goods, services, time, and talents, which are actually a much stronger form of currency than cash itself. Using your newly found creative skills, you can now put together whatever type of trade deals you want in business or life. Barter trade, in our opinion, is simply a metaphor for creative thinking.

The purpose of this chapter is to help you get ready to do your first trade, be that B2B (business to business) or C2C (consumer to consumer). In this book, we have mainly talked about B2B transactions. But the mindset is the same, be it B2B or C2C: always looking for how to make the most of overlooked and unused assets. We understand that some people will need more assistance to get started. But we hope by now that we have started to open your mind and imagination to all the possibilities, options, and opportunities that are available to you once you allow yourself to think outside the box, and to realize your true potential in ways you never knew you could!

But to move to the cashless world, you will need to make a para-

MCHUMOR.com by T. McCracken

"And they said I couldn't take it with me."

digm shift in order to break your long-standing habit (or addiction) of reaching for your wallet, checkbook, or check card every time you need to purchase something. You need to stop thinking cash and start thinking trade!

We can't promise that you will become a billionaire with your trades, like the founders of the Home Shopping Network and Carnival Cruise Lines, or that you will do a deal like Pepsi did, but we do know that by studying what is in this book very carefully, you will become an expansive and creative thinker, always looking for trade opportunities, and will start to make the most of everything you have—your time, imagination, energy, space, inventory, talents, and more. And if we are able to do this, we will have achieved the goal of this book, because we will have enriched your life!

We have not really taught you anything new in this book, but we have simply helped you remember what you have in your genes— a natural talent to trade.

BARTER IS THE ALTERNATIVE CURRENCY

Barter, as you know now, should be treated as a currency, which it really is. And it is one of the best problem-solving tools available to you in business or life.

 **INSIDE SECRET #85**

Any exchange of goods and services without exchange of money is barter.

As we pointed out, in a true barter or trade, it is illegal to exchange money.

Although you may think barter or trade only happens in developing countries, it is not true. Sure, a fish vendor in the Philippines may still today exchange his or her catch for a kilo of rice on the street; in the Western world, it is just done at a more sophisticated level.

In the Persian Gulf, oil payments for arms is the widespread currency.

In all the case studies where I put together barter-trade deals, the first thing that I would say to the merchant is, "Please keep your wallet and checkbook in the drawer; what I am about to show you will not require you to use this."

I needed to disarm my opponent first!

YOUR JOURNEY OF A THOUSAND MILES STARTS WITH THE FIRST STEP

Lao Tzu was right. The journey of a thousand miles always begins with the first step. Having been involved in barter trade for the last forty years, I have learned one thing: that people either get the concept immediately and see the power and potential and run with it, or they don't. We hope you are one of the former, because we know how much it can change and impact your life in a positive way if you embrace it. This is why we wrote this book.

LITTLE HINGES OPEN BIG DOORS. ASK!

In life or in business, what ultimately stops people is fear, and in most cases it is fear of rejection. But we always need to remember that:

Realization is always a direct result of expectation.

You usually get in life what you expect! Most people really fear that if they ask someone to trade, and they say no, they would be insulted.

As you have seen, by offering people the opportunity to trade with you, you are actually doing them a favor, as they may not be aware of all the benefits that trade offers that you do now! You can help them leverage their purchasing power very quickly once they master trade.

In the real world:

INSIDE SECRET #86

Ninety percent of the people you meet will have never considered barter trade as a currency or means of commercial transaction. This gives you a huge competitive advantage!

Most people whom you meet will not know about barter trade, and by asking them, you will be helping them immensely!

INSIDE SECRET #87

The starting point of a trade transaction is to ask, then to educate.

In every barter-trade deal that I have done, I had to ask first. Most of the people whom I dealt with had no idea what barter trade was all about (or they had the wrong idea)! They were misinformed.

You have seen how even my assistant at the radio station in New Orleans tried to convince the car dealer in New Orleans that I was taking advantage of him. Who can you trust these days?

Once you can educate people on the benefits of trade, you will find that they will quite happily want to trade with you. What you will find is:

INSIDE SECRET #88

The number-one reason why people don't trade is that they simply don't understand it!

What surprises us is how few books have been written on barter trade. There is still a lot of misunderstanding around it. This means that a lot of education is required before someone will trade with you. Common questions are:

- How will I be paid?

- When will I be paid?

- Who will pay me?

After reading this book, you should easily be able to address their concerns.

BARTER IS A SALE AND TAKES SALES SKILLS!

Because most people are not aware of barter trade, they are usually skeptical when it is mentioned. They think that they might be taken advantage of. There is certainly an amount of education that goes with a trade transaction, and it is not as simple and convenient as cash. But as you have seen, it is worth the effort.

When a barter trade transaction occurs, it is a sale just like any other sale; you just did not pay for it or receive conventional cash.

To do a barter trade, you will need to remove some of the skepticism, fear, and misunderstanding that surrounds barter.

Sales is defined by many as the art of convincing.

One of the biggest challenges of barter is selling people on the concept; to many it is just a totally new idea.

 # INSIDE SECRET #89

It takes sales skills to teach people barter trade. You are selling them on a whole new way (actually, a very old way) of doing commerce.

WHAT DO YOU DO, OR WHAT DO YOU OWN?

The starting place for trade opportunities is to take your own inventory. With your newly found trade mentality, your currency is now your time, talents, space, knowledge, products, services, etc. So you need to start thinking about how much you already have in your bank. You will really be surprised to find out how wealthy you already are!

The quickest way is to break down what you have to trade is to ask yourself,

WHAT DO YOU LIKE TO DO?

Start by answering the following questions:

- Do you have any specific talents that you know of?
- Can you do what you do for a living in your spare time?
- Have people ever told you that you are talented in anything?
- What did people say that you did best in your last five jobs?
- Have you ever entered a competition?

- Have you ever won any awards? If so, for what?
- What do people ask you to help them out with?
- What help have you provided to your family and friends?
- What do you like to do in your spare time?
- When you join a team, what do you volunteer to do?
- If you have volunteered, what did you volunteer to do?
- What keeps you awake at night and gets you up early in the morning?
- What would you do if money was not an issue for you?
- What does your spouse ask you to do on the weekends?
- What were you last complimented for?
- What are you criticized for doing too much of?

Another way may be to list all the things that fall under the following main categories:

- Time
- Products/goods
- Services
- Talents
- Space
- Skills/talents
- Equipment/use of equipment
- Contacts

The answers to the above questions give you an indication of what you have to trade! And we are sure you have a lot!

WHAT DO YOU HATE TO DO?

- What are the five things that you hate to do?

- What are the things that consume most of your time?

The answers to these two simple questions tell you what you are willing to trade for!

TURN WHAT YOU HAVE INTO WHAT YOU WANT!

We all have something that someone else needs or wants. This is why we are hired for the different jobs that we do. Some of us are good with our hands and work as carpenters, and others are good with our minds and end up as professional managers or doctors. But in all cases, we all make our living serving others.

These skills are transacted on a cash or trade basis daily. The same can be true with any product or service you have—you can transact them on a cash or trade basis also. Just start to see trade as an alternate currency.

You don't have to sell what you have in your garage at a garage sale for cash or at a massive discount. Businesses also wouldn't need to do "fire sales"—if they could find someone to trade with, they would get full retail for their product or service.

What ultimately kills most businesses is the commoditization trap, which is when they end up simply competing on price and there is no differentiation. This is not a good place to be. Trade prevents you from having to do this.

The most important thing to remember is that everything is tradable. I have traded food, gasoline, cars, pinball machines, and more. The mindset you need to have to be successful in trading is to treat trade as cash and not to compromise. If someone is willing to accept or pay you cash, they can be just as willing and able to pay you and accept cash.

HOW MUCH IS YOUR EXCESS WORTH?

Now that you know all the things you have to trade with and things you like to do, you can simply assign a dollar value to these:

Name of Skill/Talents	$ per Hour/Market Rate
Writing articles	50
Proofreading	40
Gardening	10
Legal services	200
Total:	300

In the above example, you may be a lawyer, whose passion and talents are writing articles, proofreading, and gardening. If you just have one hour of these skills available to trade per day, that would be $300 per day in monetary value in your bank ready to trade.

This is just a simple example, but it shows you how your spare time or skills are worth a lot of money, when traded.

HELLO, IS ANYONE THERE?

Once you know how much you have and you have placed a value on it, next it is time to start to trade what you have.

Start by making a list of friends, colleagues, or existing business clients who might have what you want and want what you have. We know someone who was a baker and was looking for someone to update her website regularly, so she offered her friend, who was a website designer, unlimited cakes and other baked goods to do the job. It continues to work perfectly!

Coming up blank on people you know? Try one of these more organized ways to find a match.

- **Join a local bartering club.** You can do a quick Internet search.

- **Join a time bank.** You can register (for free) at your local time bank's website and list the services you have to offer. For each hour of work you provide to another member, you earn a "time dollar," redeemable for any service someone else has listed on the site. Find a time bank in your area, or learn how to start your own, at timebanks.org. Time banks are wonderful, as they remove the biggest fear people have, which is asking people if they will trade! The people in the time bank are already interested in trading with you! (See below for more on time banks.)

- **Conventional marketing.** You can run ads in the local classifieds, use an online list like craigslist, or use word of mouth.

BANK YOUR TIME NOW BEFORE YOUR BANK ACCOUNT SHRINKS!

Across America, we are now seeing a grassroots movement of people who have decided not to wait for Washington, DC, or Wall Street to bail us out of the current economic condition we are in. This movement is called "time banks."

A time bank is a place where you simply deposit and withdraw time instead of money, all online. This is growing very rapidly as a community-based support network. You sign up and list your skills and things you would like to help with (e.g., painting, typing, driving, etc.). When someone in the network requires help in your field, you will be contacted and asked to do the job. The person who requested the help will be debited the time and it will be credited to your account.

For example, you may sign up and indicate plumbing as one of your skills. Mrs. Smith requires some plumbing, you provide the service, and it takes you 1.5 hours to complete the job. Mrs. Smith is debited 1.5 hours, and you will be credited 1.5 hours. You now have 1.5 hours to use if needed.

A few weeks later, you need help with your garden, so you go online and request help. Mr. Gardner comes to do your gardening for you, and it takes him 1 hour to do the job. You will be debited 1 hour, and Mr. Gardner is credited 1 hour.

Time bank communities are growing across the United States. Check out a time bank in your local area (www.timebank.org). If you need a will, you can simply take your local lawyer's dog for a walk!

You may not have the spending power, but you do have the time! So it is best to grow your time bank, before your real bank account shrinks!

YOU WERE BORN TO TRADE!

To continue to keep you in the trade mindset, we are now going to present to you some real-world examples of what is possible with this mindset.

There Is Such a Thing as a Free Lunch!

If you are an editor or writer for a magazine, you can approach any business and offer to write a review in exchange for their product or service, which could be legal, hairstyling, food, etc.

This is not bribery, but a simple value-for-value exchange—and a win-win for both parties. Magazines and newspapers are always looking for good content. And all local businesses need publicity and advertising.

Share in the Profits!

Businesses are a perfect place to find the best trade opportunities. Any independent professional can trade their time for a percentage of profits. You may be a web designer, a lawyer, a copywriter, or a graphics designer. You can approach any business and offer to do work for them for a percentage of profits, or incremental profits, as a result of your work. For this type of transaction to happen, you simply need to apply Marketing 101: "Find a need and fill it."

Research local businesses, find out what you think they are lacking, and offer this service as a barter-trade deal.

Fix Up Your House for Free!

If you have a spare room in your house, you can offer it to a handyman, and in return he or she can fix up your house on the weekends. I know some people who have had this arrangement for years! They took their 5,000-square-foot, $600,000 property in San Francisco and both extended and renovated it over four years. It is now it is 10,000 square feet and worth $3 million. This was all done using a simple trade arrangement—accommodation for services—without a penny changing hands! Yes, they became millionaires in the process.

Carpool for Any Service You Need!

If you have kids, you are probably already in the barter-trade business, as you most likely at some time have traded carpooling services with a neighbor or friend. This is simply your time for their time. But if you don't have kids, you could just as easily trade your carpooling services for something else, like resume writing. So if you are unemployed, and you know someone in your neighborhood who is good at writing resumes and has kids, you can easily trade your time to carpool for them in return for resume writing services.

Start Your Acting Career Using Trade!

Like any business, shopping centers thrive on traffic. If you have a talent that can attract crowds, you can try to negotiate some space outside a major shopping center. They get the traffic; you get to test your talents!

Meet the Cashless Man

Is there such a thing as moneyless living? Yes! Cash is so ingrained in us that we associate cash with security. We are actually addicted to cash. And our biggest fear in life is that if we do not get any cash, we would cease to exist in our modern-day economy and die. But it is simply not true. It is possible to live without having any cash.

Mark Boyle in the UK spent an entire year without cash, cards, or anything, and shows us how he did it in a book called *The Money-less Man: A Year of Freeconomic Living* (Oneworld, 2010). He totally gave up his relationship with the conventional money system during his final semester of a business and economics degree he was completing in Ireland, when he stumbled upon a DVD about Gandhi. Gandhi's famous message was, "Be the change that you wish to see in the world."

The first step for him was to find a form of sustainable shelter. For this he turned to a project called Freecycle, through which he located a caravan that someone else didn't want any more. He then needed somewhere to put this new home, so he decided to volunteer three days a week at an organic farm near Bristol, England, in return for a place to park his caravan.

Having no means of paying bills, his next challenge was to set up his home to handle utilities. For heating, he installed a wood-burning stove that he had converted from an old gas bottle, using a flue pipe he had salvaged from the recycle centers. He fueled it using wood from trees he cut down on the farm.

A local member of the Freeconomy community (the alternative economy he founded in 2007) then showed him how to make a "rocket stove" from a couple of old olive-oil catering tins that were destined for the landfill. This meant that for the next twelve months, he had to cook outside, while feeding the stove with broken-up old vegetable boxes. He said that observing wildlife taught him much more about nature than any documentary he had seen on the television.

The one thing he did spend money on (about £360) before beginning the experiment was a solar panel to supply him with enough electricity for a light, his laptop, and his phone (on which he could only receive calls).

He had a compost toilet made from old pallets from a nearby hardware store. As for toilet paper, he took newspapers from local Bristol newsagents. He jokes that it was double-quilted, but it quickly seemed normal.

He washes in a river or under a solar shower and rarely uses soap, but if he does, he uses a home-grown soapwort. For toothpaste he uses a mixture of cuttlefish bone, which gets washed up on the UK's shores, and wild fennel seeds.

Food? On the organic farm, he grows his own food: potatoes, beans, kale, carrots, salads, root vegetables, squash, onions, etc. He is also able to secure waste food and other goods from local restaurants and shops. Many food chains discard food prior to its expiration date, and this provides a good resource for Mark.

In fact, he organized a free mini-festival called the Freeconomy Feast 2009, where he and a BBC chef fed two hundred fifty people a three-course meal with full service for free, completely out of waste food!

The final leg of his food table is bartering—using his skills or any excess food he produces to secure any need not met by the other three methods.

He cycles thirty-six miles roundtrip to Bristol to collect items he needs. He says that although this takes a lot more time and energy than driving or catching the bus or train, it's also an economical alternative to his old gym subscription, and he finds cycling much more enjoyable than using motorized vehicles.

He points out that he would much rather have his time consumed making his own food outdoors than watching some reality TV show in a so-called "living" room. Where money once provided him with a primary sense of security, he now finds it in friends and the local community. His closest friends are the people he meets, because he had to build real relationships based on trust and kindness, not money.

A fascinating story. Mark is a true environmentalist and a good economist. We are not asking you to do what Mark Boyle did. But he shows us that if we really wanted to, we could live without cash. It is our fear and sense of security that holds us back.

You can learn more about the Free Economy at http://www.free-economy.org/. This is a free service in which you can give away goods and services for free, and look for them as well. At its most basic level, it is a charity; at its most sophisticated, it is a cashless gift economy in which supply and demand is linked by information networks.

The purpose of the Free Economy is to help people and to relieve stress on the environment. They believe that it is possible to live in an economy in which the needs of others are respected as much as your own, and in which things are done more for what they are than what you can get out of them.

Again, we are not asking you to do what Mark did, but we are asking you to open your mind and heart to barter trade. We think you will be pleasantly surprised.

Raise Money for a Charity Using Trade

Most charities raise money through fund drives, dinners, etc. Now that you have the barter mindset, you really don't want people's money; you would rather have their time! And most people usually have more spare time than they do money! You can use this to your charity's advantage. You can raise money for your favorite charity by simply asking people to volunteer their time instead of their money. And in most cases, people would be willing to do this.

If you approached one hundred people and asked them to give you one hundred dollars, most would kindly refuse your offer. But if you asked them to offer you one hour of their time, 90 percent would probably say yes. It does not cost them anything, and most people usually have a few hours a day when they are not doing anything.

Now let's say of the one hundred people, 90 percent are professionals: bestselling authors, consultants of some kind, tax attorneys, health coaches, etc. These are the types of services that are much prized.

You could now go to a trade club and deposit these trades for other services for your charity, such as building services to extend your local religious establishment. Or you may want to simply cash out by going to a local radio station and start offering these services at 50 percent of what people would normally pay. You now know how cash conversion works.

One of our fellow traders had traded with Hawaiian Airlines and received a large chunk of Hawaiian Airlines tickets. He then put them on the radio, offering $89 for return flights to Hawaii. The station got 3,600 calls in one minute, which actually blew out the phone lines to the station! He was taking cash conversion to the limit!

So if you are able to get credits for people's time rather than their money, you can then auction them off at whatever price you want, since you have not paid anything for it!

As you can see, trade deals are only limited by your imagination. It basically boils down to what skill you have and who needs it.

TRADE VERSUS CASH: THE FINAL CONFLICT

This whole book has been about barter trade, and how to use trade to leverage your marketing spend—and you have seen numerous examples of how this is done. But before we set you loose to trade, we want to ensure that you understand how trade and cash work hand-in-hand with each other.

Both trade or cash only have one goal, and that is to improve the quality of your life.

Trade is ideal when there are excess products and services that cannot be sold for cash, when there is everything to gain and nothing to lose. In most of the case studies I (Dave) shared with you, I traded media for things that people thought were useless, including excess cabins on Carnival Cruise Lines, out-of-date Chryslers, old acoustic guitars, etc. What made it mindblowing was being able to take something that people thought was worthless and use it as currency, without any discounts, and get full value for them. So trade is ideal for unused, out-of-date, excess, or spare capacity that cannot be sold for cash. In these cases, it's time to get trade back on your radar.

However, trade, with all its power and potential, is unlikely to ever become mainstream again. We're unlikely to return to a complete barter system, because for this to happen, everyone would have to be willing to accept a trade. So the statement "cash is king" still has merit. But trade is a smart way to both save and generate cash.

Trade has its time and place. The ideal time is when you cannot sell what you have for cash. But it's also true that if you trade for what you want versus pay cash, you will always save.

You have seen how trade provides you with immense benefits, including unlimited purchasing power, allowing you to get what you want right now, paying at a steep discount sometime in the future, and more. But this all depends on finding someone to trade with, either directly or through a trade club. We hope that this book has provided you with the education, knowledge, and insight to not only start trading, but help you in educating people you plan to do trade deals with.

Again, even with all its immense power, we don't believe that trade will ever replace cash; it simply supplements cash transactions. But:

 # INSIDE SECRET #90

You should always offer trade as part of any transaction that you do with anyone. Whatever portion they trade with you is the portion that will provide you with economic benefit.

You have seen in all the case studies how trade can produce explosive growth and results. Our advice is that if you can get cash, take it. But always make it a habit to ask for trade as part of any transaction that you may do.

Trading today still represents a very small percentage of all commercial transactions, which is both good and bad. It is good, as you clearly have the opportunity to offer trade with many people who are used to doing commerce only on a cash basis. But it is bad because you are up against an environment that is used to doing commerce with cash, due to its convenience and universality.

So barter trade is a tool, just like any other tool, that can be used to perform a specific function. It is certainly smart to take unproductive assets or excess time, inventory, products, or services and use them to get something very useful.

In the case of the media, they are always happy to trade for what you may conventionally define as useless. The media are businesses too, and they have excess/unused airtime that can be used to acquire products or services that they can cash-convert at any time, or give away as prizes for a competition. Most of the case studies that we presented to you in chapter 6 are examples of this.

Trade should be used as part of any business transaction, because both parties benefit and gain from a barter trade deal, like in the jeweler and TV case study. But there are just not enough people who understand trade, nor is there a large enough global trade community. Trade clubs are on the rise, but still account for a very limited amount of world trade. So you have to create a customized trade deal, using some form of triangulation, if you really want a specific deal.

Trade is a tool to (1) conserve cash, since it does not use it, and (2) generate cash through cash conversions. And you can use this tool as necessary.

 **INSIDE SECRET #91**

At the end of the day, all barter-trade deals should be/are converted to cash. This is because cash is more universal and is accepted at more places than trade.

But don't just trade for the sake of trading. You should trade because you have something that you don't need or use and want to use it for something that you need or want.

INSIDE SECRET #92 (It's huge!)

Always look to use trade as a tool to gain leverage and then convert your trade to cash to give you universal buying power. Just like in poker: you are going to have to cash in your chips sometime, once the game's over!

We hope that you have enjoyed our time together. You now have the insight, knowledge, and expertise to perform trades. Barter trade brings back the traditional way of doing business, which is about helping people solve everyday problems.

Trade is really good for our planet, as it forces us to recycle and reuse what we have. So you could say that trade is part of "going green." Remember, Goodwill Industries estimates that 23.8 billion pounds of clothing and textiles end up in US landfills every year! And that is just in the United States alone. If you add to that all the other excess inventory, like cars, household furniture, etc., by getting involved in trade, you are also helping our planet for future generations.

We hope that you now understand why Albert Einstein said, "If I had to live my life all over again, I would elect to be a trader of goods rather than a student of science. I think barter is a noble thing."

I think, like you, he had finally figured it out!

FINAL INSIDE SECRET #93!

What is said about you will become your reputation and brand. To be a good trader, always ensure fair trade; always deliver on your promise. Trading can be a very lucrative business, and word will get around very quickly about what type of trader you are!

Good luck! Focus on doing your first deal quickly, however small it is, and other deals will soon come your way. We are sure that you will find barter trade both fun and creative. It is not only a way for us to help each other, but to become less wasteful in our habits, learn to use everything that we have, and help our planet by recycling, reusing, and regenerating our assets, creativity, and knowledge. Please keep in touch with us at www.nocashnoproblem.net

THINGS TO REMEMBER FROM THIS CHAPTER

- Barter trade will require you to break your age-old habit of reaching for your wallet or checkbook.

- Every time you do a transaction, always ask if people will trade with you a portion of the transaction.

- Most people you meet will never have heard of trade, and you will have to educate them.

- Take inventory of everything you have: time, talents, space, etc., and then use barter as a means to recycle them!

- Barter will never replace cash, but it provides a viable alternative.

chapter ten
—— 10 ——
Getting Started

The happiest people in the world are not those who
have everything, but those who make the most of
everything they have.

Anonymous

For more information on how to get started, visit www.nocash-noproblem.net, or contact Dave or Ali directly:

DAVE AT:
2360 NE Coachman Rd
Clearwater, FL 33765
Phone: 727.424.4991
Dave@Wagenvoord.com
Fax: 727.441.1300

LOLA AT:
Phone: 727.510.7622
lola@tantalk1340.com

ALI AT:
masterpervez@gmail.com

ORDER THE AUDIO BOOK FOR JUST $99!

Order the audio book *No Book? No Cash? No Problem!* Listen in firsthand as Jay Abraham, the world's greatest marketing expert, interviews Dave Wagenvoord. In a grueling 3.5 hours covering "inside barter secrets," you will hear Dave talk in more detail about the case studies mentioned in this book.

You can download immediately for $99 by going to www.nocash-noproblem.net. The normal retail price of the audio training is $299! Or you can contact Dave directly if you would like CDs.

"If you were a tree,
which one would you want to end up as?"

DAVE'S GUARANTEE

If after listening to the audio book you don't save or make ten times the cost, contact Dave Wagenvoord for a full immediate refund. And of course, you still get to keep the audio training. Dave can be contacted at 727.424.4991 or at Dave@Wagenvoord.com.

about the authors

---- ★ ----

ABOUT DAVE WAGENVOORD

Dave is the president of Wagenvoord Advertising, owner of several radio stations, and one of the greatest barter experts in the world. He has personally bartered at least $500 million worth of goods and services, including exotic travel, capital goods and equipment, luxury cars, electronics, homes and condominiums, and even entire businesses. Dave has been a featured speaker at Jay Abraham's marketing seminars.

Here are just a few of some of his amazing barter feats:

- He traded 900 Chrysler Imperials in six weeks. Only 1,100 were manufactured that year.

- He traded 16,000 guitars for Yamaha for more than $2,000,000 worth of radio advertising.

- He traded $5,000,000 worth of DHL Air Courier credits for television in a matter of months.

- He traded for advertising on hundreds of radio stations for ten years for Carnival Cruise Lines.

- He built Channel 26 TV in New Orleans, which is now owned by the Chicago Tribune.

- He owned the Peter Lawford home on the beach in Santa Monica that was used by President Kennedy and known as the "Western White House." This was originally built as the home of Louis B. Mayer, the founder of Metro-Goldwyn-

Mayer, and is the birthplace of the concept of the Academy Awards. Dave traded for the house and much of its contents.

- He purchased a radio station in Northern California and paid 60 percent of the down payment in the furniture trade credits.

- He bought $1,000,000 worth of network airtime from a bankruptcy court in one of the wildest and most profitable "little" barter deals of all time.

- His clients have included:

Best Western Hotels	Avis	Carl's Jr
Sheraton Hotels	Hawaiian Tropic Sutan Oil	Mutual Broadcasting
Outrigger Hotels	Costa Cruise Line	Levitz Furniture
Beverly Wilshire Hotel	Regal Cruise Line	General Rent-A-Car
L'Ermitage Hotel Beverly Hills	Pearl Cruise Line	Coty Perfume
Carnival Cruise Line	Aer Lingus airlines	Aeroflot
Aero Mexico	Royal Caribbean Cruise	Carnival Airlines
KLM	Silver Club Hotel Reno Nevada	Wittenauer Watches
Continental Airlines	Mexicana Airlines	Landmark Hotel Las Vegas
RCA	Air France	Hawaiian Air
Citizen Watches	Curtis Publishing	Surf Resorts Hawaii
Turner Broadcasting	Lufthansa Air	MGM Grand Las Vegas
NBC Radio	TWA	Sahara Hotel Las Vegas
Budget Rent-A-Car	Samsung	Eton Radios

And Over 5,000 radio and TV stations in America

Dave has been actively trading, avidly arranging, and brokering high-dollar barter transactions for over forty years and is probably the shrewdest and quickest-witted business person you will ever meet.

Contact Dave at:

2360 N.E. Coachman Road

Clearwater, FL 33765

Phone: 727.424.4991

Web: Dave@Wagenvoord.com

Fax: 727.441.1300

Contact Lola at:

Phone: 727.510.7622

lola@tantalk1340.com.

You can listen to our programming on the web at tantalk1340.com (Tampa Bay) or KLRG-AM 880 and FM 94.5 (Little Rock) at KLRG880.com.

All our stations are news, talk, and sports and can be heard worldwide. Your comments and input regarding our programming are always welcome. Let us hear from you.

Do You Want to Do a Deal with Dave?

If you have excess merchandise or products that you would like to convert to an advertising credit or liquidate for cash, and that are valued from $50,000 to $50 million, contact Dave.

ABOUT ALI PERVEZ

Ali Pervez is one of America's leading marketing educators, with over twenty-five years of hands-on, practical global marketing experience.

He is the bestselling marketing author of Get Your Black Belt in Marketing (www.blackbeltinmarketing.com). He holds undergraduate and postgraduate degrees in science, and he was awarded an MBA with a distinction project in marketing from Manchester Business School in the UK. He was also awarded two Vice President awards for Outstanding Contribution in Marketing within his first year at Abbott Laboratories. He is a Fellow of the Royal Society of Chemistry, founder of The Black Belt Marketing Consulting Group, and a much-sought-after international marketing consultant.

If your organization is looking to implement formal marketing systems, he may be contacted at masterpervez@gmail.com.

Other books by Ali Pervez include:

MARKETING IS KING!

This book covers Marketing 101.

www.marketingisking.com

GET YOUR BLACK BELT IN MARKETING

This book covers how to use marketing to grow your sales.

www.blackbeltinmarketing.com

Printed in the USA
CPSIA information can be obtained
at www.ICGtesting.com
JSHW022322140824
68134JS00019B/1237